AESCHYLUS I

THE COMPLETE GREEK TRAGEDIES

Edited by David Grene & Richmond Lattimore

THIRD EDITION *Edited by Mark Griffith & Glenn W. Most*

AESCHYLUS I

THE PERSIANS *Translated by Seth Benardete*

THE SEVEN AGAINST THEBES *Translated by David Grene*

THE SUPPLIANT MAIDENS *Translated by Seth Benardete*

PROMETHEUS BOUND *Translated by David Grene*

The University of Chicago Press CHICAGO & LONDON

MARK GRIFFITH is professor of classics and of theater, dance, and performance studies at the University of California, Berkeley.

GLENN W. MOST is professor of ancient Greek at the Scuola Normale Superiore at Pisa and a visiting member of the Committee on Social Thought at the University of Chicago.

DAVID GRENE (1913–2002) taught classics for many years at the University of Chicago.

RICHMOND LATTIMORE (1906–1984), professor of Greek at Bryn Mawr College, was a poet and translator best known for his translations of the Greek classics, especially his versions of the *Iliad* and the *Odyssey*.

The University of Chicago Press, Chicago 60637
The University of Chicago Press, Ltd., London
© 2013 by The University of Chicago

22 21 20   5

ISBN-13: 978-0-226-31143-2 (cloth)
ISBN-13: 978-0-226-31144-9 (paper)
ISBN-13: 978-0-226-31145-6 (e-book)
ISBN-10: 0-226-31143-0 (cloth)
ISBN-10: 0-226-31144-9 (paper)
ISBN-10: 0-226-31145-7 (e-book)

Cataloging-in-Publication Data is available from Library of Congress.

♾ This paper meets the requirements of ANSI/NISO Z39.48–1992 (Permanence of Paper).

CONTENTS

EDITORS' PREFACE TO THE THIRD EDITION

The first edition of the *Complete Greek Tragedies*, edited by David Grene and Richmond Lattimore, was published by the University of Chicago Press starting in 1953. But the origins of the series go back even further. David Grene had already published his translation of three of the tragedies with the same press in 1942, and some of the other translations that eventually formed part of the Chicago series had appeared even earlier. A second edition of the series, with new translations of several plays and other changes, was published in 1991. For well over six decades, these translations have proved to be extraordinarily popular and resilient, thanks to their combination of accuracy, poetic immediacy, and clarity of presentation. They have guided hundreds of thousands of teachers, students, and other readers toward a reliable understanding of the surviving masterpieces of the three great Athenian tragedians: Aeschylus, Sophocles, and Euripides.

But the world changes, perhaps never more rapidly than in the past half century, and whatever outlasts the day of its appearance must eventually come to terms with circumstances very different from those that prevailed at its inception. During this same period, scholarly understanding of Greek tragedy has undergone significant development, and there have been marked changes not only in the readers to whom this series is addressed, but also in the ways in which these texts are taught and studied in universities. These changes have prompted the University of Chicago Press to perform another, more systematic revision of the translations, and we are honored to have been entrusted with this delicate and important task.

Our aim in this third edition has been to preserve and strengthen as far as possible all those features that have made the Chicago translations successful for such a long time, while at the same time revising the texts carefully and tactfully to bring them up to date and equipping them with various kinds of subsidiary help, so they may continue to serve new generations of readers.

Our revisions have addressed the following issues:

- Wherever possible, we have kept the existing translations. But we have revised them where we found this to be necessary in order to bring them closer to the ancient Greek of the original texts or to replace an English idiom that has by now become antiquated or obscure. At the same time we have done our utmost to respect the original translator's individual style and meter.
- In a few cases, we have decided to substitute entirely new translations for the ones that were published in earlier editions of the series. Euripides' *Medea* has been newly translated by Oliver Taplin, *The Children of Heracles* by Mark Griffith, *Andromache* by Deborah Roberts, and *Iphigenia among the Taurians* by Anne Carson. We have also, in the case of Aeschylus, added translations and brief discussions of the fragments of lost plays that originally belonged to connected tetralogies along with the surviving tragedies, since awareness of these other lost plays is often crucial to the interpretation of the surviving ones. And in the case of Sophocles, we have included a translation of the substantial fragmentary remains of one of his satyr-dramas, *The Trackers* (*Ichneutai*). (See "How the Plays Were Originally Staged" below for explanation of "tetralogy," "satyr-drama," and other terms.)
- We have altered the distribution of the plays among the various volumes in order to reflect the chronological order in which they were written, when this is known or can be estimated with some probability. Thus the *Oresteia* appears now as volume 2 of Aeschylus' tragedies, and the sequence of Euripides' plays has been rearranged.
- We have rewritten the stage directions to make them more consistent throughout, keeping in mind current scholarly under-

standing of how Greek tragedies were staged in the fifth century BCE. In general, we have refrained from extensive stage directions of an interpretive kind, since these are necessarily speculative and modern scholars often disagree greatly about them. The Greek manuscripts themselves contain no stage directions at all.

- We have indicated certain fundamental differences in the meters and modes of delivery of all the verse of these plays. Spoken language (a kind of heightened ordinary speech, usually in the iambic trimeter rhythm) in which the characters of tragedy regularly engage in dialogue and monologue is printed in ordinary Roman font; the sung verse of choral and individual lyric odes (using a large variety of different meters), and the chanted verse recited by the chorus or individual characters (always using the anapestic meter), are rendered in *italics*, with parentheses added where necessary to indicate whether the passage is sung or chanted. In this way, readers will be able to tell at a glance how the playwright intended a given passage to be delivered in the theater, and how these shifting dynamics of poetic register contribute to the overall dramatic effect.

- All the Greek tragedies that survive alternate scenes of action or dialogue, in which individual actors speak all the lines, with formal songs performed by the chorus. Occasionally individual characters sing formal songs too, or they and the chorus may alternate lyrics and spoken verse within the same scene. Most of the formal songs are structured as a series of pairs of stanzas of which the metrical form of the first one ("strophe") is repeated exactly by a second one ("antistrophe"). Thus the metrical structure will be, e.g., strophe A, antistrophe A, strophe B, antistrophe B, with each pair of stanzas consisting of a different sequence of rhythms. Occasionally a short stanza in a different metrical form ("mesode") is inserted in the middle between one strophe and the corresponding antistrophe, and sometimes the end of the whole series is marked with a single stanza in a different metrical form ("epode")—thus, e.g., strophe A, mesode, antistrophe A; or strophe A, antistrophe A, strophe B, antistrophe B, epode. We have indicated these metrical structures by inserting the terms

STROPHE, ANTISTROPHE, MESODE, and EPODE above the first line of the relevant stanzas so that readers can easily recognize the compositional structure of these songs.

· In each play we have indicated by the symbol ° those lines or words for which there are significant uncertainties regarding the transmitted text, and we have explained as simply as possible in textual notes at the end of the volume just what the nature and degree of those uncertainties are. These notes are not at all intended to provide anything like a full scholarly apparatus of textual variants, but instead to make readers aware of places where the text transmitted by the manuscripts may not exactly reflect the poet's own words, or where the interpretation of those words is seriously in doubt.

· For each play we have provided a brief introduction that gives essential information about the first production of the tragedy, the mythical or historical background of its plot, and its reception in antiquity and thereafter.

· For each of the three great tragedians we have provided an introduction to his life and work. It is reproduced at the beginning of each volume containing his tragedies.

· We have also provided at the end of each volume a glossary explaining the names of all persons and geographical features that are mentioned in any of the plays in that volume.

It is our hope that our work will help ensure that these translations continue to delight, to move, to astonish, to disturb, and to instruct many new readers in coming generations.

MARK GRIFFITH, *Berkeley*
GLENN W. MOST, *Florence*

INTRODUCTION TO AESCHYLUS

Aeschylus was born sometime in the 520s BCE into an aristocratic family based in Eleusis, twelve miles to the west of central Athens. So he was a teenager when the ruling monarchical family of the Pisistratids was expelled and the first democracy at Athens was created (510–508). As well as becoming the greatest tragic playwright of his generation, Aeschylus fought against the Persians at Marathon (490), where his brother was killed, and in the sea battle at Salamis (480). He began producing plays in the 490s, won his first victory in 484, and continued writing tragedies until shortly before his death in 455. The epitaph that was written on Aeschylus' tomb (in Gela, Sicily)—allegedly composed by him and his family—mentions his service at Marathon against the Persians, but says nothing about his achievement as a playwright.

The titles of over ninety plays by Aeschylus are recorded, though only six survive that can be attributed to him with certainty (scholars are divided about the authenticity of the *Prometheus Bound* that is transmitted under his name). On several occasions he composed his plays for the annual competition to be a continuous and coherent sequence, with the three tragedies forming almost a single—very extended—three-act play, as we find with the *Oresteia*. (The fourth play of the sequence was of course a satyr-drama, usually connected thematically to the three preceding tragedies; see p. 7 below.) Unfortunately, we do not possess more than one play from any of Aeschylus' other trilogies; and we possess only small fragments from any of his satyr-plays. Some of Aeschylus' rivals likewise produced connected trilogies:

but some did not, preferring to compose three quite separate tragedies on different themes; and sometimes Aeschylus did this too, as in the case of the plays produced with his *Persians* (472). It is striking that Sophocles, who began his playwriting career in 468 BCE and for over a decade was competing against Aeschylus, seems never to have adopted the "connected" trilogy format at all; nor subsequently did Euripides.

Tragedy and satyr-drama were already well established in Athens by the late sixth century, and when Aeschylus began to produce plays he was competing against several famous rivals, most notably Phrynichus, Choerilus, and Pratinas. Almost nothing of their work survives, so it is impossible to gauge to what point the art of tragedy had advanced before Aeschylus. Some scholars have regarded him as being effectively the "creator" of Greek tragedy, but it is clear that his predecessors and rivals were highly regarded, especially for their music and choral song, and the fact that he seems to us to be such a powerful innovator may be due in part to the loss of his rivals' works. In any case, Aeschylus undoubtedly played a major role in developing tragedy to its pinnacle of dramatic sophistication and moral power, and he established himself as by far the most popular and influential of all the tragedians before Sophocles, winning thirteen first prizes in the years between 484 and 458.

Aeschylus' unique tragic style is especially remarkable for its extensive and intensive use of the chorus: some of the choral songs extend for over 150 lines each, and the variety of meters and complexity of structure and lyric registers are astonishing. His style too is bold and unconventional, with extensive use of metaphor and imagery. Aeschylus was credited by some with introducing the second speaking actor, and possibly also (late in his career) the third (though some ancient critics credited this to the young Sophocles). Another innovative move of his was to cast the chorus as leading characters in certain plays (for example, *The Suppliant Maidens* and *The Eumenides*). He also seems to have been among the first to have taken dramatic advantage of the *skênê* building: the *Oresteia* is the first surviving drama to contain scenes that require three speaking actors on stage simultaneously; and the positioning of the Watchman on the roof in *Agamemnon*, and the frequent references throughout the trilogy to the "door" and to entrances in and out of the "house" or "temple," are unprecedented in earlier plays.

Aeschylus is said to have visited Sicily at some point during the 470s as the guest of Hieron, ruler of Syracuse and Acragas, and to have composed and presented plays there. But he appears to have been resident in Athens for most of the rest of his life, producing plays about Achilles and Patroclus, about Pentheus and Dionysus, about Niobe, about Ajax, Philoctetes, and the death of Hector (all themes popular also with later tragedians), and others too, in addition to those trilogies of which parts or all survive to the present: *The Seven against Thebes* (467), *The Suppliant Maidens* (probably 463), and his masterwork, the *Oresteia* (458). The date, and even the authenticity, of the Prometheus trilogy (of which *Prometheus Bound* survives complete, as well as several fragments of *Prometheus Unbound*) are very uncertain: these issues are discussed further in the introduction to that play. Within a year of producing the *Oresteia*, Aeschylus left Athens for another visit to Sicily, and died there in 456 or 455.

We know nothing about the personality or lifestyle of Aeschylus, though we do know that one of his sons, Euaion, was a renowned beauty, as well as being a playwright and actor of distinction. The other son, Euphorion, was also a very successful tragedian, and the family continued to flourish in the world of Athenian theater throughout the fifth and fourth centuries. Aristotle and other ancient sources report that Aeschylus was an initiate of the Eleusinian Mysteries in honor of the goddesses Demeter and Persephone, and that he was once prosecuted for revealing secret aspects of the Eleusinian Mysteries in one of his plays—but was acquitted. Scholars both ancient and modern, while viewing such stories with some degree of skepticism (since ancient "biographies" of poets tend to be wildly fanciful and unreliable), have generally agreed that Aeschylus' plays consistently display a serious and challenging engagement with religious matters, though they disagree as to whether specifically Eleusinian and eschatological elements can be identified.

After his death, Aeschylus' reputation continued to flourish. His sons doubtless helped to keep his plays in the public eye; and an ancient tradition (perhaps not trustworthy) states that the Athenians passed a special decree allowing Aeschylus' plays to be revived at the annual festival, an honor granted to no other deceased playwright. One way or another, some of his plays clearly did continue to be performed and to be read, at least by the highly educated, since allusions and parodies are frequently found in the plays of Euripides and Aristophanes. When Aristophanes came to write the *Frogs*, shortly after the death of Euripides in 405, he presented the clash between old and new tragedy as a contest between Aeschylus and Euripides. In the quotations and parodies that abound in that comedy, Aeschylus' style is consistently represented as being "grandiloquent," high-flown to the point of obscurity or bombast, and geared to maintaining the dignity and solemnity of the tragic genre, as against Euripides' modernizing tendencies and introduction of more everyday issues, unpoetic language, and low characters.

During the fourth century, Aeschylus' plays, along with those of Sophocles and Euripides but no other Athenian tragedians, were acknowledged as classics and as being especially worthy of being preserved and performed—though it seems that by this date there was little concern for keeping whole trilogies together (plays instead were catalogued alphabetically), and also a diminishing interest in satyr-plays. A more or less complete collection of Aeschylus' plays was made in Alexandria during the third century BCE, and even though Aeschylus' plays were generally regarded as being less accessible and enjoyable than Sophocles' and especially Euripides'—because of Aeschylus' more archaic language, large amounts of choral lyric, and limited opportunities for actors and rhetoricians to exploit the argumentative and ethical dimensions of the characters' speeches—all three tragedians were read in both Greek and Roman schools throughout antiquity.

Scores of fragments from Aeschylus' plays, mostly quite short, are found in quotations by other authors and in anthologies from the period between the third century BCE and the fourth century CE; but they are far fewer and less extensive than the fragments of Sophocles or (especially) Euripides; and the same is true of papyrus finds. So while Aeschylus remained a classic both in the schools and among later practitioners of the dramatic art (including Naevius, Ennius, Accius, Pacuvius, and Seneca in Rome), familiarity with his work at first hand seems to have become increasingly limited, even in the schools. Some of his plays certainly were much better known than others, and the selection of seven plays that we possess was probably made in the second century CE: from that point on, the other plays ceased to be copied and thus eventually were lost to posterity. At Byzantium (Constantinople, today Istanbul), three plays in particular were most widely copied, the triad consisting of *Prometheus Bound*, *The Seven against Thebes*, and *The Persians*. The other four plays fell into almost complete neglect, and two of them (*The Suppliant Maidens* and *The Libation Bearers*) are preserved in only one manuscript copy. It is sobering to realize that without this one manuscript, we would not possess the complete *Oresteia* trilogy.

Aeschylus' reputation in the modern era has rested almost entirely on the seven plays that survive in our medieval manuscripts. During the Renaissance and Enlightenment periods, his plays were still relatively little read and seldom performed. Things changed when German and British Romantic poets and intellectuals of the eighteenth and nineteenth centuries began to pay more attention to archaic Greek literature and to aspects of Hellenic culture that had for long been regarded as "primitive" or crude. Aeschylus became the object of increasing admiration and study, for his arresting and large-scale religious questioning, his powerful presentation of moral and political problems, his musical and ritualistic energy, and his sheer linguistic exuberance and density. Since the nineteenth century, indeed, his plays have been regarded as the foundation stones of Western drama. The *Oresteia* has always been by far the most widely read and often staged, though *Prometheus Bound* has also been influential with progressives and revolutionaries of various hues. Aeschylus' reputation continued to grow throughout the twentieth century, especially because of his challenging representation of gender conflict and sociopolitical crisis; his plays have been more widely read and staged, decade by decade, and nowadays he stands unchallenged as the true "father of Greek tragedy."

HOW THE PLAYS WERE ORIGINALLY STAGED

Nearly all the plays composed by Aeschylus, Sophocles, and Euripides were first performed in the Theater of Dionysus at Athens, as part of the annual festival and competition in drama. This was not only a literary and musical event, but also an important religious and political ceremony for the Athenian community. Each year three tragedians were selected to compete, with each of them presenting four plays per day, a "tetralogy" of three tragedies and one satyr-play. The satyr-play was a type of drama similar to tragedy in being based on heroic myth and employing many of the same stylistic features, but distinguished by having a chorus of half-human, half-horse followers of Dionysus—sileni or satyrs—and by always ending happily. Extant examples of this genre are Euripides' *The Cyclops* (in *Euripides*, vol. 5) and Sophocles' *The Trackers* (partially preserved: in *Sophocles*, vol. 2).

The three competing tragedians were ranked by a panel of citizens functioning as amateur judges, and the winner received an honorific prize. Records of these competitions were maintained, allowing Aristotle and others later to compile lists of the dates when each of Aeschylus', Sophocles', and Euripides' plays were first performed and whether they placed first, second, or third in the competition (unfortunately we no longer possess the complete lists).

The tragedians competed on equal terms: each had at his disposal three actors (only two in Aeschylus' and in Euripides' earliest plays) who would often have to switch between roles as each play progressed, plus other nonspeaking actors to play attendants and other subsidiary characters; a chorus of twelve (in Aeschylus' time) or fifteen (for most of the careers of Sophocles and Euripides), who would sing and dance formal songs and whose Chorus Leader would engage in dialogue with the characters or offer comment on the action; and a pipe-player, to accompany the sung portions of the play.

All the performers were men, and the actors and chorus members all wore masks. The association of masks with other Dionysian rituals may have affected their use in the theater; but masks had certain practical advantages as well—for example, making it easy to play female characters and to change quickly between roles. In general, the use of masks also meant that ancient acting techniques must have been rather different from what we are used to seeing in the modern theater. Acting in a mask requires a more frontal and presentational style of performance toward the audience than is usual with unmasked, "realistic" acting; a masked actor must communicate far more by voice and stylized bodily gesture than by facial expression, and the gradual development of a character in the course of a play could hardly be indicated by changes in his or her mask. Unfortunately, however, we know almost nothing about the acting techniques of the Athenian theater. But we do know that the chorus members were all Athenian amateurs, and so were the actors up until the later part of the fifth century, by which point a prize for the best actor had been instituted in the tragic competition, and the art of acting (which of course included solo singing and dancing) was becoming increasingly professionalized.

The tragedian himself not only wrote the words for his play but also composed the music and choreography and directed the productions. It was said that Aeschylus also acted in his plays but that Sophocles chose not to, except early in his career, because his voice was too weak. Euripides is reported to have had a collaborator who specialized in musical composition. The costs for each playwright's production were shared between an individual wealthy citizen, as a kind of "super-tax" requirement, and the city.

The Theater of Dionysus itself during most of the fifth century BCE probably consisted of a large rectangular or trapezoidal dance floor, backed by a one-story wooden building (the *skênê*), with a large central door that opened onto the dance floor. (Some scholars have argued that two doors were used, but the evidence is thin.) Between the *skênê* and the dance floor there may have been a narrow stage on which the characters acted and which communicated easily with the dance floor. For any particular play, the *skênê* might represent a palace, a house, a temple, or a cave, for example; the interior of this "building" was generally invisible to the audience, with all the action staged in front of it. Sophocles is said to have been the first to use painted scenery; this must have been fairly simple and easy to remove, as every play had a different setting. Playwrights did not include stage directions in their texts. Instead, a play's setting was indicated explicitly by the speaking characters.

All the plays were performed in the open air and in daylight. Spectators sat on wooden seats in rows, probably arranged in rectangular blocks along the curving slope of the Acropolis. (The stone semicircular remains of the Theater of Dionysus that are visible today in Athens belong to a later era.) Seating capacity seems to have been four to six thousand—thus a mass audience, but not quite on the scale of the theaters that came to be built during the fourth century BCE and later at Epidaurus, Ephesus, and many other locations all over the Mediterranean.

Alongside the *skênê*, on each side, there were passages through which actors could enter and exit. The acting area included the dance floor, the doorway, and the area immediately in front of the *skênê*. Occasionally an actor appeared on the roof or above it, as if flying. He was actually hanging from a crane (*mêchanê*: hence *deus ex machina*, "a god from the machine"). The *skênê* was also occasionally opened up—the mechanical details are uncertain—in order to show the audience what was concealed within (usually dead bodies). Announcements of entrances and exits, like the setting, were made by the characters. Although the medieval manuscripts of the surviving plays do not provide explicit stage directions, it is usually possible to infer from the words or from the context whether a particular entrance or exit is being made through a door (into the *skênê*) or by one of the side entrances. In later antiquity, there may have been a rule that one side entrance always led to the city center, the other to the countryside or harbor. Whether such a rule was ever observed in the fifth century is uncertain.

THE PERSIANS

Translated by SETH BENARDETE

THE PERSIANS: INTRODUCTION

The Play: Date and Composition

Aeschylus' *Persians* is the earliest surviving Greek tragedy. It was first performed in 472 BCE, as part of a tetralogy made up of plays on quite different themes. We know the titles of the other three plays, though the plays themselves have been lost except for fragments: *Phineus*, *Glaucus of Potniae*, and the satyr-drama *Prometheus Fire-Kindler*. All three were on mythological subjects, and it appears they had little in common. So in this particular year Aeschylus followed the pattern that was more usual with other tragedians, including Sophocles and Euripides, of composing four quite separate plays as his entry into the competition, rather than a tightly connected tetralogy like the *Oresteia*. The production won first prize.

We are informed by ancient sources that the play was performed at least once in Sicily, a year or two after its first performance in Athens, at the request of the ruler of Syracuse, Hieron. We do not know whether Aeschylus rewrote the play for this performance or adapted it to take into account the Sicilians' victory over Eastern invaders (the Carthaginians), which occurred on almost the same date as the Athenian victory over the Persians at Salamis; and, if so, which version we possess today.

The Story

The idea of basing a tragic drama on a recent historical event, rather than on traditional myth, may seem surprising to modern readers; but it was apparently not so unusual in the early decades of tragic competition in Athens. In fact Aeschylus' celebrated predecessor and rival, Phrynichus, had previously produced a tragedy, *The Phoenician Women*, on exactly this same theme; and an ancient scholar quotes the first line of Phrynichus' play to demonstrate that Aeschylus' whole play was heavily dependent on it.

The momentous events of 480-479 BCE were of course well known to all Greeks; and the Athenians had played a central role in them. King Xerxes of Persia had led an enormous invading force of troops and ships into Greece. Athens had been evacuated and occupied by the invading forces, but in an amazing reversal, Athenian ships had crushingly defeated the Persian navy and thereby ruined the Persian strategy of a combined land and sea operation to take over the rest of the mainland. Xerxes himself had watched the crucial sea battle off the island of Salamis, just a few miles from the city of Athens. Afterward, a considerable contingent of the Persian forces, including Xerxes, returned home, leaving a large army to continue the campaign on land. The next spring (479) this army was in turn resoundingly defeated by Greek forces led by the Spartans, at the battle of Plataea. Thus the Persians had for a second time in a decade been repelled (the first time had been Darius' much smaller assault, defeated by Athenian infantry at Marathon in 490), and the independence of Athens and other Greek city states had been preserved.

These events immediately acquired a status in the Greek national consciousness comparable to the capture of Troy, or the exploits of Theseus and Heracles—eminently suitable material for tragic drama. At the same time, it would hardly be appropriate for a living Greek man to be made the central focus of a tragedy: instead, Aeschylus followed the example of Phrynichus and set his play in the Persian court, with the main focus on the royal family. Nonetheless, this tragedy concentrating on the disastrous turnaround of the Persian king's fortunes was obviously at the same time a celebration of Athenian success in particular and of Greek discipline and values in general.

The action of Aeschylus' play takes place in front of the tomb of King Darius at the palace in Sousa, Persia's capital city. The chorus of Persian elders (a body of senior advisers to the royal family) begins by anxiously discussing the status of the expedition that left to invade Greece several months earlier, led by King Xerxes himself. Then the queen (not named in the play, though we know from Herodotus and from Persian documents that this is Atossa, widow of Darius and mother of Xerxes) arrives to talk with them, and tells them of an ominous dream she has had. A messenger arrives, announcing the catastrophic defeat at Salamis and narrating in detail the loss of Persian lives and ships, including the painful and costly march of retreat through northern Greece. The queen and chorus are devastated, but also relieved to learn that Xerxes is safe and returning home, though his clothing is in shreds (from mourning) and his spirit broken. The chorus, at the queen's suggestion, now conjures up the dead spirit of King Darius, Xerxes' father, from his tomb. Darius expresses disapproval and disappointment at his son's failure, and goes on to predict the impending defeat at Plataea. After Darius' ghost returns to the underworld, and the queen also departs to prepare to greet her son, Xerxes himself arrives, and the final scene consists of a long lyric lament, sung in antiphonal exchange between the chorus and their king.

Aeschylus' play is the earliest extant account of the events of the Persian Wars: the much more extensive and detailed narrative of Herodotus in his *Histories* was not composed until some forty years later. But the play was never intended to accurately represent historical reality. Although it has plenty of oriental coloring (costumes, exotic wailing and dancing, self-abasement of the chorus in the presence of royalty), for the most part the Persians speak like Greeks and observe largely Greek customs and religion. The resounding lists of foreign names are colorful but not very authentic. The scale of the massacre of Persian troops on land that is described as the culmination of the slaughter at Salamis (lines 441–71) seems to be greatly exaggerated. The references to Darius' unblemished military record are somewhat fanciful, and Xerxes' entry on foot in the final scene, with torn clothing and minimal retinue, suggests a degree of catastrophe and humiliation far removed from the actual Persian experience.

Instead of historical authenticity, Aeschylus sought and achieved brilliant dramatic impact, especially through such striking effects as the queen's dream, the apparition of the ghost of old king Darius, the pathos of Persian loss and bewilderment, and the elaborate incantations and lamentations of the chorus.

After Aeschylus' *Persians*, we do not hear of any further stagings of tragedies depicting recent historical events in the fifth-century Athenian theater. Certainly neither Sophocles nor Euripides ever wrote such a play. We do not know why this change of fashion occurred. By contrast, in the Roman theater, historical dramas constituted a flourishing genre, with *Octavia* (attributed, wrongly, to Seneca) a sole surviving example.

Transmission and Reception

Beyond the play's reperformance in Sicily, *The Persians* continued to be well known in Athens throughout the fifth century, and Herodotus must have known the play, though he makes little obvious use of Aeschylus' particular themes or language. At the end of the century, the exotic flavor of Aeschylus' music and choreography in the play is mentioned approvingly in Aristophanes' *Frogs*, and the innovative musician and poet Timotheus drew extensively from it in his own *Persians* (of which a substantial fragment survives on papyrus). In the Hellenistic period, the Jewish playwright Ezekiel likewise adapted episodes from Aeschylus' play for his *Exodus* (*Exagogê*). But for the most part, it was Herodotus' account of Xerxes' invasion and the Persian royal court that was best known and most influential for later writers and composers.

In general, Aeschylus' plays were much less widely read in ancient schools or for pleasure than the plays of Sophocles or (especially) Euripides. Most of them gradually ceased to be copied and faded into oblivion. When the time came to make a selected edition of seven Aeschylean plays (at some point in the Roman period, perhaps for school use), *The Persians* was included, doubtless because of its ever-topical subject matter—the defeat of an Eastern threat and the humiliation of an overly ambitious ruler. The play survived into the Byzantine and Renaissance eras and, along with *The Seven against Thebes* and *Prometheus Bound*, made its way into the triad of Aeschylean plays that were copied frequently from the twelfth to the fifteenth century. As a result, some of the manuscripts of the play contain quite extensive marginal comments (scholia).

Since the Renaissance, plays and operas loosely based on *The Persians* have been fairly common, though Herodotus and the late antique *Alexander Romance* have generally been much more influential. A number of operas titled *Xerxes* were composed during the seventeenth and eighteenth centuries: most bear little resemblance to Aeschylus' play. Much closer to Aeschylus' tragic vision are T. Maurice's *Fall of the Mogul* (1806) and Percy Bysshe Shelley's *Hellas* (1821), written during the period when Greece was fighting for independence against the Ottoman Empire.

Since the 1920s *The Persians* has been performed in all parts of the world. Often the political allegory has been overt, with Xerxes suggesting a Nazi or Soviet or domestic dictator, or implying a warning to the contemporary US as an overreaching imperialist power. Sometimes "Eastern" music and performance style has been incorporated in imaginative ways. Notable productions include those of Dimitri Rondiris for the Greek National Theater (1939, 1958, 1967), Karolos Koun with the Theatro Technis (1965–67), Mattias Braun (1960s), the Berliner Ensemble (1961, 1972, 1983), Peter Sellars (1993), and Ellen McLaughlin (1995).

Both in adapting and in interpreting this tragedy, theater practitioners and critics have been divided as to whether Aeschylus was aiming to flatter the Athenians by celebrating their military and cultural superiority over the luxurious, feminized "other" of the East, or was sympathetically exploring the disastrous effects on any community of an unnecessary war caused by an impetuous and overly ambitious leader. The truth is doubtless that he was doing both.

THE PERSIANS

Characters   CHORUS of Persian elders
             QUEEN of Persia (Atossa), widow of Darius, and
             mother of Xerxes
             PERSIAN MESSENGER
             GHOST OF DARIUS
             XERXES, king of Persia

Scene: *The palace of Xerxes at Sousa; in the foreground the tomb of
Darius.*

                              (Enter Chorus from the side.)

CHORUS [*chanting*]
> *Of the Persians gone*
> *to the land of Greece*
> *here are the trusted:*
> *as protectors of treasure*
> *and of golden thrones.*
> *We were chosen by Xerxes—*   5
> *emperor and king,*
> *son of Darius—*
> *in accord with age,*
> *guards of the country.*
> *For the king's return*
> *with his many-manned troops*
> *doom is the feeling*
> *in my heart convulsed,*   10
> *as it faces the future.*

For all Asia is gone,
its strength and its youth:
and the women lament for their men.°
To the city of Persians
neither herald nor horseman returns.   15
And some have left Agbatana
and some Sousa and
ancient Cissa,
both on horse and on ship
and on foot displaying
legions of battle: 20
Artaphrenes, Megabates,
Astaspes, Amistres,
leaders of Persians, kings
who are slaves of the greatest of kings,
guarding the legions they rush,   25
both as bowman and knight,
with their temper resolved,
fearful in aspect,
dreadful in battle;
and exultant in horses
Artembares, and Masistres,   30
and the brave archer Imaeus,
and Pharandakas,
and the driver of horses
Sousthenes.
And others were sent
by the nourishing Nile:
Egyptian-born Sousiscanes,
Pegastagon, great Arsames   35
ruler of sacred Memphis;
and Ariomardus
governing ancient Thebes;
and those who dwelling by marshes
are rowers of ships,
skillful and countless.

And the Lydians soft   40
who inhabit the coast
follow commanders and kings:
Metrogathes and brave Arcteus,
and golden Sardis sent   45
many charioteers,
with horses by twos and by threes,
fearful the sight to behold.
And the neighbors of Tmolus—
they threaten to yoke
in servitude Hellas;   50
and the Mysian lancers,
Tharybis, Mardon,
anvils of battle;
and golden Babylon
pours forth her crowds—
borne by their ships—
who in drawing the bow   55
rely on their boldness.
And the tribes from all Asia
who carry the saber
follow beneath the
awesome parade of their king.
Thus of the Persian land
of her men the flower is gone,   60
nursed by the earth, and all Asia
laments, consumed by longing;
and parents and wives
counting the days
tremble at lengthening time.

[singing]

STROPHE A

The destroyer of cities now,   65
that kingly army, has gone
over the strait to the land

on linen-bound pontoons;
tightly was clamped the Way
of Helle, Athamas' daughter, 70
as the neck of the sea was yoked.

ANTISTROPHE A

And the furious leader drives
the herd of populous Asia, 75
wonderful over the earth.
And admirals stern and rough
marshals of men he trusts:
gold his descent from Perseus,
he is the equal of god. 80

STROPHE B

In his eyes lazuli flashing
like a snake's murderous glances,
with his mariners, warriors, many,
and his Syrian chariot driving,
hard on the glorious spearmen 85
the archer Ares he leads.

ANTISTROPHE B

To the great torrent of heroes
there is none worthily equal,
who resist, by defenses secured,
the unconquerable billows of ocean: 90
Persians are never defeated,
the people tempered and brave.

STROPHE C

For divine fate has long prevailed,°
enjoining Persians to wage wars 95 (103)
which destroy towers and ramparts,
along with glad tumult of horsemen,
and cities overthrown.

ANTISTROPHE C

Later, when the vast ocean was foaming,

[22] AESCHYLUS

whitened by the boisterous winds,　　　　　　　　　100 (111)
they learned, trusting to cables
and to pontoons which convey men,
to cross the sacred sea.

EPODE

Deceitful deception of god—
what mortal man shall avoid it?
With nimbleness, deftness, and speed　　　　　　　105 (95)
whose leaping foot shall escape it?
Benign and coaxing at first
it leads us astray into nets which
no mortal is able to slip,
whose doom we never can flee.

STROPHE D

Thus clothed in black my heart is torn,　　　　　　115
fearful for those Persian arms:
lest the city hear, alas!
that reft of men is Sousa;

ANTISTROPHE D

and lest the city of Cissa shall,　　　　　　　　　120
with crowds of women crying,
sing antiphonal, alas!
and rend their garb of mourning.　　　　　　　　125

STROPHE E

All the horse and infantry,
like a swarm of bees have gone
with the captain of the host,
who joined the headlands of either land,　　　　　130
crossing the yoke of the sea.

ANTISTROPHE E

Beds with longing fill with tears,
Persian wives in softness weep
each her bold warrior husband　　　　　　　　　135
dispatched with gentle love and grief,

[23] THE PERSIANS

as they're left alone in the yoke.

[chanting again]
But come, Persians, 140
let us in this ancient palace sit,
and deep and wisely found our thoughts:
How does King Xerxes fare, Darius' son?
How fare his people? Has arrows' hail 145
or strength of spear conquered?
        But look, she comes,
a light whose splendor equals the eyes of gods, 150
the mother of our king: I kneel.
Now all must address and salute her.

               (Enter the Queen from the palace, with attendants.)

CHORUS LEADER [now speaking]
O most majestic Queen of Persians, in ample folds adorned, 155
hail, aged mother of Xerxes! Consort of Darius, hail!
Consort of the god of Persians, mother of a god you are,
unless the fortune of our army brings us now a change.

QUEEN
Leaving my gold-clad palace, marriage chamber
of Darius and of myself, 160
his queen, I've come. Care quite grates my heart;
I fear, my friends, though not fearful for myself,
lest great wealth's gallop trip prosperity—
exalted by Darius and some god—
in its own dust. But, unexpectedly, 165
that dread has doubled: sums of cowardly
wealth do court contempt, and indigence
quenches ambition's flame, even if there's strength.
Though wealth we have unstinted, yet I fear
for my precious eye, Xerxes, whose presence here
I count the palace's eye. So things stand thus. 170
Advise my reason, Persians, old sureties:
all my gains with your counsel lie.

O Queen of Persia, be assured that never
twice do you have to tell us word or deed
which our willing strength can guide; for we
are loyal, whom you call your counselors.   175

QUEEN

With frequent, constant, and nocturnal dreams
I have lived, ever since my son, gathering
his army, departed, his will to pillage Greece;
but never a more vivid presence came
than yesternight's.   180
Into my vision it seemed two women came,
one decked out in Persian robes, the other
in Dorian, both of them flawless and impressive,
excelling in beauty any who live today.   185
Sisters they were, and inheriting their father's land,
one received Greece, the other Asia to dwell.
Then strife arises between them, or so I dreamed;
and my son, observing this, tries to check   190
and soothe them; he yokes them to a chariot,
bridles their necks: and one, so arrayed, towers
proud, her mouth obedient to reins;
but the other stamps, annoyed, and rends apart
her trappings with her hands; unbridled, seizes   195
the chariot and snaps its yoke in two.
My son falls; his father, Darius, pitying,
stands by his side—but at his sight Xerxes
tears his robes. Thus in the night these visions   200
I dreamed: but when, arisen, I touched the springs'
fair-flowing waters, approached the altar, wishing
to offer sacrifice religiously
to guardian deities, whose rites these are,
then to Phoebus' hearth I saw an eagle fleeing.   205
Dumb in dread I stood: a falcon swooped
upon him, its wings in flight, its claws plucked

at his head: he did no more than cower, hare-like.
Those were my terrors to see, and yours to hear.   210
My son, should he succeed, would be admired;
but if he fails, Persia cannot hold him
to account. Whichever comes, safe returned, sovereign
he shall still rule.

CHORUS LEADER
                        Queen mother, excessive fear   215
or confidence we do not wish to give you.
If your dreams were ominous, approach
the gods with supplications; pray that these
be unfulfilled, and blessings be fulfilled
for you, your son, your city, and your friends.
Next you must pour libations to the Earth   220
and the dead; and beg Darius, of whom you dreamed,
to send those blessings from the nether world
to light, for you and for your son; and to hide
in darkness evils contrary, retained
within the earth. Propitious be your prayers.
We, prophetic in our spirit, kindly,
counsel you thus: and we judge that all will prosper.   225

QUEEN
Ah, loyally have the first expounders answered
my dreams; and may these blessings ripen
for my son and for our house as well!
All, as you enjoin, I'll sacrifice
to the gods and friends below, as soon as I
return to the house. But one thing more I wish   230
to know, my friends: where is Athens said to be?

CHORUS LEADER
Far from here, toward the dying flames of sun.

QUEEN
Yet still my son yearned to track it down?

CHORUS LEADER
Then all Hellas would be subject to the king.

QUEEN
So rich in numbers are they? 235

CHORUS LEADER
       So great a host
as dealt to Persians many miseries.

QUEEN
Are bow-plucked shafts their main armament?°

CHORUS LEADER
No; spears wielded close and panoply of shields.

QUEEN
What else besides? Have they sufficing wealth?

CHORUS LEADER
Their earth is veined with silver treasuries. 240

QUEEN
Who commands them? Who is shepherd of their host?

CHORUS LEADER
They are slaves to none, nor are they subject.

QUEEN
But how could they withstand a foreign foe?

CHORUS LEADER
Enough to vanquish Darius' noble host.

QUEEN
We mothers dread to calculate. 245

CHORUS LEADER
But soon you'll know all: a Persian runner comes,
bearing some fresh report of good or ill.

             (Enter Persian Messenger from the side.)

O cities of Asia, O Persian land,
and wealth's great anchorage!
How at a single stroke prosperity's 250
corrupted, and the flower of Persia falls
and is gone. Alas! the first messenger of woe,
he must disclose entire what befell:
Persians, all the barbarian host is gone. 255

CHORUS [*singing in this interchange with the Messenger, who speaks in reply*]

STROPHE A

O woe! woeful evil,
novel and hostile.
Alas! Persians weep
hearing this woe,
unexpected.

MESSENGER

How all has been destroyed, and I behold 260
the unexpected light of my return!

CHORUS

ANTISTROPHE A

Oh, long seems our aged
life to us elders,
alas! hearing woe
Unexpected. 265

MESSENGER

And since I was witness, not merely subject to rumor,
I can indicate what sorrows came.

CHORUS

STROPHE B

Woe upon woe, in vain
the crowd of missiles, massed,
came from Asia to Greece. 270

MESSENGER

The lifeless rotting corpses glut the shore
and adjacent fields of Salamis.

CHORUS

ANTISTROPHE B

Woe upon woe, of friends   275
the sea-dyed corpses whirl
vagrant on craggy shores.

MESSENGER

The bow protected none, but all the host,
defeated in the naval charge, was lost.

CHORUS

STROPHE C

Raise a mournful, doleful cry   280
for Persians wretched:
all they made, all woe.
Alas! the host destroyed.

MESSENGER

O most hateful name of Salamis!
O woe! how I groan recalling Athens.   285

CHORUS

ANTISTROPHE C

Athens hateful to her foes.
Recall how many
Persian women are widowed,
and mothers have lost their sons.

QUEEN

Long am I silent, alas! struck down   290
by disasters exceeding speech and question.
Yet humans must perforce endure misfortunes
that are sent by the gods. Speak, disclose entire
what befell, quietly, though you grieve.   295

Who did not die? For whom of the captains
shall we lament? Whose sceptered death drained his ranks
    manless?

MESSENGER
              Xerxes himself lives to behold the light.

QUEEN
  O for my palace you spoke a greater light,   300
  and after blackest night a whiter day!

MESSENGER
  But Artembares, captain of ten thousand
  horse, was dashed against Silenia's
  rugged shore; and satrap Dadakes,
  spear-struck, did lightly tumble from his ship;   305
  and native-born Tenagon, the bravest
  Bactrian, still haunts sea-buffeted
  Ajax' isle; and Lilaeus, Arsames,
  and Argestes, conquered near the island
  where doves do thrive, now butt their heads on the rocks;   310
  and the neighbors of Egyptian Nile-waters,
  Adeues, Arcteus, and, third, shielded
  Pharnouchus, from a single ship
  were drowned; and Matallus, satrap of Chrysa,
  dying, leader of a thousand horse,
  changed to richest red his thickset flowing
  beard, and dipped his skin in crimson dyes;   315
  and Magian Arabus and Bactrian
  Artabes, all aliens in a savage
  country, perished; Amphistreus, who wielded
  the much-belaboring spear, and Amistres,   320
  brave Ariomardus, all made Sardis weep;
  and Mysian Seisames, Tharybis,
  commander of five times fifty ships,
  his race Lyrnaean, handsome to look upon
  (his fortune was not so), dead he lies;   325
  Syennesis too, the leader of Cilicians,

who taxed the enemy with toil above all others,
has died, nobly. So many of the rulers I
recall, but of the many woes, report
but few.   330

QUEEN
                    Alas! I hear the greatest
of misfortunes, shame of Persians, and shrill
lament. But tell me, returning to your tale,
what was the total number of Greek ships,
that thought themselves a match for Persian arms   335
in naval combat?

MESSENGER
                    Had numbers counted,
the barbarian warships surely would have won;
the Greeks but numbered thirty tens, and ten
apart from these a chosen squadron formed.   340
But Xerxes led—and this I know full well—
a thousand, of which seven and two hundred
ranked supreme in swiftness. The count stood so.
Seemed we unequal to you? Some deity destroyed   345
our host, and weighting down the balance swung
the beam of fortune. The gods saved the city
of the goddess Pallas.

QUEEN
                    What? Athens still
stands unsacked?

MESSENGER
                    As long as there are men
the city stands secure.

QUEEN
                    What was the beginning   350
of disaster? Tell me. Who began?
The Greeks? My son—exultant in his numbers?

    Either an avenger or a wicked
god, my Lady (whence it came I know not)
began the whole disaster. From Athenian
ranks a Greek approached, addressing Xerxes   355
thus: "When the gloom of blackest night
will fall, the Greeks will not remain, but leap
to their rowing benches, and each by secret course
will seek to save his life." And he your son,   360
upon hearing this, in ignorance of the Greek
man's guile and the jealousy of gods,
harangued his captains publicly: "As soon
as sunlit rays no longer burn the earth
and darkness sweeps the quarters of the sky,   365
rank the swarm of ships in three flotillas:
have them guard the entrances, the straits' sea-pound;
and girdle others round Ajax' island.
And if the Greeks escape their evil doom,
contriving secret flight, all your heads   370
will roll. I warrant it." So he spoke
in confident pride: of the god-given future
he knew nothing. So, having eaten, they set
themselves in order, each heart obedient,   375
and each sailor looped the thong about his oar.
When the glare of sunlight died, and night
came on, every rower was at his oar,
and each marine took up his proper weapons.
Rank encouraged rank, and longboats sailed   380
to the stations each had been assigned.
All night the captains kept the fleet awake;
and night ran on. Yet no Greek army set
secret sail: and when the steeds of day,   385
white and luminous, began to cross
the sky, a song-like, happy tumult sounded
from the Greeks, and island rocks returned   390
the high-pitched echo. Fear fell among us,

deceived in hope; for they (and not as if to flee)
chanted a solemn paean, and to battle
rushed with fervent boldness: trumpets flared,   395
setting every Greek aflame. At once
concordant strokes of oars in roaring eddies
slapped the waters' depths: soon we saw
them all: first the right wing led in order,   400
next advanced the whole armada.
A great concerted cry we heard: "O Greek
sons, advance! Free your fathers' land,
free your sons, your wives, the sanctuaries
of paternal gods, the sepulchers
of ancestors. Now the contest's drawn: 405
all is at stake!" A babel of Persian tongues
rose to meet it: no longer would the action
loiter. Warships struck their brazen beaks
together: it was a Greek ship that began
the charge, as a Phoenician vessel's stern   410
was smashed; then others drove against each other.
At first the floods of Persians held the line,
but when the narrows choked them, they could not help
each other, but smitten by each others' prows,   415
they shattered their oars entirely on the bronze.
The Greek warships, calculating, dashed
round and encircled us; ships showed their bellies:
no longer could we see the water, charged
with ships' wrecks and with the blood of men.   420
Corpses glutted beaches and the rocks.
Every warship urged its own escape
in anarchic rout. And meanwhile the enemy
with broken bits of oars and splintered wreckage
were clubbing and spiking our men in the water   425
like tunny or some other catch of fish.
Moans, shrieks, and cries of lamentation
possessed the open sea, until the black
eye of evening, closing, hushed them. The sum

of troubles, even if I should rehearse them
for ten days, I could not exhaust. Rest   430
assured: never in a single day
so great a number died.

QUEEN

Alas! a sea of troubles breaks in waves
upon the Persians and barbarian tribes.

MESSENGER

But what we've told would scarcely balance woes   435
untold: misfortune came upon them, which
swung the beam to weigh them double these.

QUEEN

But what greater hatred could fortune show?
What misfortune came upon the soldiers,
to tilt the scale of troubles even further?   440

MESSENGER

All those Persians who were in nature's prime,
excellent in soul and nobly bred to grandeur,
always first in trust, met their death
in infamy, dishonor, and in ugliness.

QUEEN

Oh, wretched am I, alas! What catastrophe   445
destroyed them?

MESSENGER

There is an island fronting Salamis,
small, scarce an anchorage for ships,
where the dancer Pan rejoices on the shore;
there Xerxes sent those men to kill   450
any shipwrecked enemies who sought the island
as a refuge (for easily, he thought,
the Greek army would be overcome);
he also bid them rescue friends. He judged
the future badly. For when god gave the Greeks

the glory of sea victory, that same day,   455
now armed in bronze, they leaped ashore, and drew
the circle tight around the island. Thus
surrounded, our men had nowhere they could turn.
Many rattled to the ground, whom stones
had felled, and others killed by arrows, shot   460
from bowstring; and then in a final rush
the Greeks came at them, hacking, mangling their limbs,
until the life of every single one
was gone.
        Xerxes wailed, beholding the lowest depths   465
of woe. Seated on a hill that near
the sea looked over all his host, he ripped
his robes and poured out piercing lamentation;
then dispatched his regiments on land: they fled
orderless. Now you may lament their fate   470
added to the others' summed before.

QUEEN

O hateful deity! how you deceived
the Persians! Bitter was the vengeance
which my son at famous Athens found:
she could not sate her appetite with those
whom Marathon had made the Persians lose.   475
For these my son, exacting as requital
punishment (or so he thought),
called on himself so numerous
a train of woes. Tell me, what ships escaped?
Where are they now? Can you clearly tell?

MESSENGER

The captains of the remaining ships set sail   480
before the wind, fleeing in disorder;
but the land army perished in Boeotia:
some in want of water, racked with thirst,
while others, gasping emptily on air,
crossed to Phocis, Locria, the Malian   485

Gulf, where Spercheian waters kindly drench
the plain; and thence Achaea and Thessaly
received us, starving: it was there most died   490
in hunger and in thirst: both we felt.
To Magnesia and Macedonia we came,
the River Axius, the reedy marsh
of Bolbe, the mountain Pangaeon,
and Thrace. There in the night a god   495
roused winter out of season, and froze solid
the stream of holy Strymon: all who had
believed the gods were naught now sang their prayers,
making obeisance both to Earth and Sky.
When the army finished its many invocations   500
to the gods, it started crossing over the ice.
And whoever set out before the sun god's rays
spread and scattered in the sky, this man
was safe. But soon the brilliant orb of sun,
its rays aflame, melted the river's midst;   505
one man fell on the next; happy he whose breath
of life was cut short quickest! The survivors
did make their way—but painfully—through Thrace
and have arrived at last to hearth and home,   510
few out of many. Thus the city of Persians
may lament, regretting the loss of dearest youth.
Truthful I have been, but omit many
of the woes a god has hurled against the Persians.

(Exit Messenger to the side.)

CHORUS LEADER
O deity so full of toil and trouble!   515
How heavily you leaped upon all Persia!

QUEEN
Ah! woe is me, the army all destroyed.
O bright night's spectacle of dreams,
how clearly you foresaw my miseries,

and you, my counselors, how poorly you have judged.   520
But yet, as you have counseled thus,
first to the gods I'll offer prayer; and then
to Earth and the dead I'll come to offer gifts
from the house, a rich libation. I know I pray
for what is done and gone, but a brighter   525
fortune, in time to come, may there yet be.
And you, worthy of trust, exchange worthy counsel;
my son, should he return before my own
return, comfort and escort him home: 530
I worry that to woes he'll add more woe.

(Exit Queen into the palace.)

CHORUS [*chanting*]
   O Zeus, King, you destroyed
   the multitudinous, proud
   host of the Persian men;
   and the cities of Sousa   535
   and of Agbatana
   you've buried in darkness of grief.
   Many with delicate hands
   rending their veils,
   drenching their breasts,
   swollen with tears,
   sharing their woe.   540
   The ladies of Persia
   softly are weeping,
   desiring each
   him to behold
   wedded but lately;
   forsaking their couches,
   soft with their coverlets,
   the joy of their youth,
   now they lament their sorrows,   545
   insatiate, full of woe.
   And I recite the mourning song,

doom of the gone,
woe upon woe.

[*singing*]

STROPHE A

Now all Asia
desolate, void,
sighs lament:
Xerxes led,   550
alas,
Xerxes lost,
O woe,
Xerxes heedless all discharged
with ocean argosies.
Why was Darius so long without harm,   555
archery's captain of citizens,
loved lord of Sousa?

ANTISTROPHE A

Armies, navies
lazuli-eyed,
linen-winged
warships carried,   560
alas,
warships destroyed,
O woe,
warships smashed with their rams driven by Greek hands.
Scarcely escaped was the leader alone
(so we have heard) in the Thracian   565
plains, wintry paths.

STROPHE B

They of the first death,
alas,
left by necessity,
woe,
round by Cychraean shores,
Oh,

moan in your anguish,
cry to the heavens your grief,
Oh, 570
wail long-weeping
mournful cries.

Torn in the sea-swirl,
alas, 575
mangled by voiceless
woe,
fish of the unstained sea.
Oh,
houses deprived grieve, 580
childless, to heavens their loss.
Oh,
elders mourning,
hear all woe.

They throughout the Asian land
no more will Persian laws obey, 585
no more the lordly tribute pay
exacted by compulsion;
nor falling faceward to the earth,
will they make obeisance now:
lost is the kingly power. 590

Nay, no longer is the tongue
kept in check, but loose are men
when loosened is the yoke of power,
to shout aloud their liberty.
And Ajax' island, soaked with blood 595
its earth, and washed round by the sea,
holds the remains of Persia.

(Enter the Queen from the palace, carrying offerings.)

QUEEN

> My friends, if one's experienced in troubles,
> one knows that, when a flood of evil comes,
> we tend to fear for everything; but when 600
> a god provides an easy voyage, we think
> that fortune's never-changing wind will blow
> forever. So now, to me all things are full of fear
> and visions from the gods assail my eyes,
> and my ears already ring with cureless songs: 605
> thus consternation terrifies my sense.
> Therefore I departed from the palace,
> returning here, unaccompanied
> by chariots, by pomp and ceremony:
> to the father of my son I bring
> libations, propitious offerings for the dead; 610
> some sweet white milk taken from a cow
> unblemished; glowing honey from the flower-
> working bee, with liquid droplets of a maiden
> stream are mingled; and this elixir
> of an antique vine, whose mother is 615
> the wild field; and golden-green the fruit
> of fragrant olive trees, always flourishing
> their leafy age; and plaited flowers, children
> of the fecund earth. Over these libations,
> the honors that I lavish on the gods below,
> my friends, recite your hymns and incantations: 620
> summon Darius' great spirit to return.

CHORUS [chanting]

> *O Queen of the Persians,*
> *honored lady,*
> *to the dark chambers*
> *libations pour;*
> *while we with our songs* 625
> *will request from the gods,*
> *who conduct the dead souls*

from the world below,
to be kindly and help.
　　You sacred divinities
dwelling below,
Earth and Hermes
and King of the Shades,
conduct his spirit 630
back up to the light
from the world of the dead!
He alone of all mortals
might know some remedy,
and show us the end of our troubles.

[*singing*]

Does he hear, the blessed king
equal to god,
as I pronounce now
resonant chantings,
barbarous, mournful, 635
clear and diverse?
Miserable sorrows I shall cry out.
Below does he hearken?

Earth and the other gods, 640
leaders of the dead,
let him arise thence,
glorious spirit, god of the Persians,
Sousa his mother;
send up the man whom,
never surpassed, 645
the Persian land buried.

Loved is the man, loved his tomb
hiding his loving ways.

Aedoneus, spirit conductor,
may Aedoneus release him 650
and send to us King Darius. Ah!

ANTISTROPHE B

Never by war wasted his men,
never in foolish ruin.
Called a god in wisdom 655
by Persians, and god-wise he was,
ruling his people well. Ah!

STROPHE C

Pashah, ancient pashah,
appear on the height of your tomb,
raise your saffron-dyed slipper, 660
reveal the peak of your royal crown.
Come to us, Father Darius, Oh!

ANTISTROPHE C

Hear the recent sorrows, 665
O master of masters, appear!
A deadly gloom hovers around us;
all the youth has perished now. 670
Come to us, Father Darius, Oh!

EPODE

Ah! Ah!
O much-lamented by your friends in death,
my lord, my lord, what does this mean,° 675
this twofold failure?
All the ships of this land
with triple banks of oars
are gone, gone. 680

(The Ghost of Darius appears.)

DARIUS

O faithful followers, companions
of my youth! O Persian counselors!

What burden's burdening the city, and why
is the earth groaning and beaten, all furrowed up
by fingernails? Anxious, I saw my wife
beside my tomb, and graciously received   685
her offerings; and you lament now, standing
at my tomb, with cries for resurrection
calling piteously. Ascent is not so easy.
The chthonic deities more readily
receive than give; but I, a potentate   690
among them, came. Be quick, that I be un-
reproached for being late. What recent woe
weighs now so heavily upon the Persians?

CHORUS [*singing*]

STROPHE

I feel awe to behold you,
I feel awe to address you,   695
whom I feared in time past.

DARIUS

Since I have risen obeying your lamentations
don't lengthen your account, but speak succinctly,
recounting everything. So lay aside
your reverence toward me.

CHORUS [*singing*]

ANTISTROPHE

I tremble to please you;   700
I tremble to tell you
what is hard to tell friends.

DARIUS   (*To the Chorus.*)

Well, since this ancient fear obstructs your sense,

                                     (*Turning now to the Queen.*)

you, aged consort of my marriage,
noble Queen, cease weeping and tell me clearly.   705
All human beings suffer human troubles;

and many woes arise, some from the sea,
and others from the land, to those who live
a longer span of life.

QUEEN
O King, who in your happy fate exceeded
mortal happiness! For while you still 710
beheld the light of sun, you spent your life
in enviable happiness, like god's;
and now I envy you your dying too,
before you had to see this depth of woe.
Everything, Darius, you will hear
succinctly: all of Persia is destroyed.

DARIUS
How? A lightning bolt of hunger? Civil 715
strife within the city?

QUEEN
No, but all
the host's destroyed at Athens.

DARIUS
Who among
my sons was leader of the troops? Tell me.

QUEEN
Furious Xerxes, who drained the country manless.

DARIUS
By foot or warship was his vain attempt?

QUEEN
By both: a double front of doubled hosts. 720

DARIUS
But how did so great an army cross the water?

QUEEN
Devices yoked the Strait of Helle and made
a pathway.

DARIUS

        He accomplished that? To close
the mighty Bosphorus?

QUEEN

        So it was; some god
laid hold of him.

DARIUS

        Ah, yes! a great divinity   725
must have deceived his sense.

QUEEN

        And one can see
the evil end he brought about.

DARIUS

        So what befell
them all, so that you thus lament?

QUEEN

        The navy,
destroyed, destroyed the troops on land as well.

DARIUS

Complete destruction by the spear for all?

QUEEN

Yes, Sousa groans for emptiness of men.   730

DARIUS

Ah! The goodly host and brave defenders!

QUEEN

All the Bactrians destroyed, no youth remains.°

DARIUS

Oh! What youth of allies has he ruined!

QUEEN

Xerxes alone, with just a few they say . . .

Ended how? Any hope of his survival?   735

QUEEN

... safely came to the bridge that joined the lands.

DARIUS

Saved, and reached our continent? Is this true?

QUEEN

Yes, a clear report without dispute.

DARIUS

Ah, that prophecy was quick to act!
Zeus hurled against my son its fulfillment,   740
while I had been praying that many years would pass
before the gods would make an end; but when
a man is young and eager, god joins in.
     So now a fountain of troubles has been found
for all those that I care for; and my son
is the one who has discovered it, in ignorance.
He hoped, in youthful confidence, to check
the sacred waters of the Hellespont   745
by chains, as if it were a slave. He smoothed
the army's way, yoking the Bosphorus
with hammered shackles. Mortal though he was,
in folly he thought to master all the gods,
including Poseidon. Wasn't his mind diseased?   750
     So now I fear the wealth I labored so
to acquire will fall the prey of conquerors.

QUEEN

From wicked men advising thus, young Xerxes
eagerly learned; they said you acquired great wealth
by warfare, while he, in cowardice, played
the warrior at home, and multiplied   755
by nothing his ancestral wealth. Thus often
these wicked men reproached him. So he planned
this warlike expedition against Greece.

DARIUS

So his deed is done, great and unforgettable!
Never had anyone before made this city   760
Sousa so empty and so desolate,
since Zeus, our lord, bestowed that honor:
one man to wield the scepter of authority
over all of Asia, rich in flocks.
First was Medus leader of our people;   765
next his son fulfilled the office well,
whose reason was the helmsman to his spirit;°
third was Cyrus, fortunate, whose rule
brought peace to all he cared for: he acquired
the Lydian people and the Phrygians too,   770
and marched his might against all of Ionia:
no god resented him, for he was wise;
and fourth to rule the land was Cyrus' son,
while fifth was Mardus, the one who shamed his country   775
and ancestral throne; but worthy Artaphrenes
(aided by guile) and his noble friends
whose task this was, slew him in his palace,
and I was with them too. I drew the lot
to rule the empire; and I often led   780
a mighty host, but never did I cast
so great a woe upon my city. Xerxes,
my son, as young in age as sense, ignored
all my instructions. Know this well, my comrades
like in age to me: of all who've held   785
these powers, none has caused such sufferings.

CHORUS LEADER

To what end, my lord Darius, do you press
these words of yours? How could we, the Persian people,
fare the best in future?

DARIUS

        If you lead
no expedition to the land of Greece,   790

not even if the Median force be greater;
for the Greek soil itself is their own ally.

CHORUS LEADER
What do you mean by that, "their own ally"?

DARIUS
Their land starves to death excessive numbers.

CHORUS LEADER
But, be sure, we'll raise a well-equipped   795
and chosen army.

DARIUS
But even they, who now
remain in Greece, shall find no safe return.

CHORUS LEADER
What? Shall not all the Persian host return
across the Strait of Helle?

DARIUS
Few of many,   800
if the oracles of gods are credited:
as we gaze at what has passed, there are no half-measures
in the outcome of the prophecies—either all
or none come true. In which case, he has left,
behind in Greece, trusting his empty hopes,   805
chosen numbers of his host, now stationed
where Asopus floods the plain and gives rich nurture
for Boeotian crops; there they'll suffer soon
the lowest depths of woe, as final payment
for insolent acts and godless arrogance.
Invading Greece, they felt no awe or reverence;
they did not hesitate to plunder images   810
of gods and put their temples to the torch;
altars were no more, and statues of divinities
were uprooted and torn right off their bases
in utter confusion. Thus having acted wickedly

they now no less are suffering in return;
and other woes the future holds in store.
For still the fount of evils is not quenched.
It wells up, and overflows: so great will be   815
the sacrificial cake of clotted gore
made at Plataea by the Dorian spear.
And corpses, piled up like sand, shall witness
mute, even to generations to come,
before the eyes of men, that never, being
mortal, ought we to cast our thoughts too high.   820
Insolence, once blossoming, will bear
its fruit, a tasseled field of doom, from which
a deadly harvest must be reaped, all tears.
Behold the punishment of these! Remember
Greece and Athens! Lest anyone disdain   825
his present fortune, lusting after more,
and end up squandering great prosperity.
Zeus is the chastener of overboastful
minds, a grievous corrector. Therefore advise
my son, admonished by reason, to be wise   830
and cease his overboastful temper from
sinning against the gods. And you, aged
mother of Xerxes, go to the palace;
gather up rich and brilliant clothes, and go
to meet your son; for he, in grief, has rent
his embroidered robes to shreds. Gently soothe   835
him with your words: to yours alone he'll listen.
Now I shall descend to the darkness below.

    Elder counselors, farewell, and though   840
in time of troubles, give your hearts each day
some pleasure: wealth can't benefit the dead.

(Exit the Ghost of Darius.)

CHORUS LEADER
    Ah, many the woes upon us and the woes
    still to come have grieved me hearing them.

O god! How many sorrows move against me!   845
But one torment bites me deepest of all,
to hear how such dishonor holds my son's
body and its robes. So I shall go
to gather proper clothing, and try to meet
him as he comes. When evils fall on those   850
we dearly love, never shall we betray them.

(Exit the Queen into the palace.)

CHORUS [*singing*]

STROPHE A

Oh! What a great and a good way of life was ours,
civilly ordered, as long as the aged
ruler of all,
sure and unconquerable king,   855
equal to god,
Darius ruled the land.

ANTISTROPHE A

Glorious arms we displayed, and the bulwarks of custom
all they did guide.° And returning from battle   860
grief had we none,
victors, unburdened of all,
happy and glad,
to home again we came.

STROPHE B

For many the cities he sacked never crossing the Halys,   865
nor leaving his hearth to rush forth.
At the mouth of the River Strymon,
near Thracian places,   870
the islands of Achelous,

ANTISTROPHE B

the cities beyond the Aegean, surrounded by towers,
obeyed him our lord, and who round
the broad Strait of Helle were dwelling,   875

and recessed Propontis,
and the gateway of Pontus

and the islands along the headland washed by the sea   880
lying close to shore:
Lesbos and Chios and Samos the olive-planted,
Paros and Naxos and Mykonos,   885
and Tenos the neighbor of Andros.

And the islands in the midst of the sea he ruled:
Ikaros and Lemnos,   890
Rhodos and Knidos and cities of lovely Cyprus,
Paphos and Soli and Salamis,   895
whose mother city's cause of all these sorrows.

Thus the wealthy and populous cities of Greeks,
the Ionian province, he ruled;   900
and the strength of his helmeted men
was unwearied, with innumerable allies.
But now all too clearly we bear god-given reversals   905
in war, overcome by these blows from the sea.

(Enter Xerxes alone, from the side.)

XERXES [*chanting*]
Oh, oh, what misery! Hateful my fate,
how unexpected,   910
how savagely swooped the deity
on Persia's people! What will befall me?
My limbs give way as I see these aged citizens.
Zeus! Would that death had covered me too   915
with the Persians gone!

CHORUS [*chanting*]
Oh alas, king, for the brave host,
and the great honor of Persian rule,   920

for the ranks of men whom a god has slain.

[*singing*]
Nations wail their native sons,°
who by Xerxes were killed
and now cram Hades;
many heroes, Persia's bloom, 925
archers, thick array of men,
myriads have perished.
Oh, oh, king of noble strength,
cruelly, cruelly Asia has to kneel. 930

XERXES [*singing until the end of the play in a lyric interchange with the Chorus, which sings in reply*]

STROPHE A

Here am I, ah, most lamentable:
to my native and ancestral land
I've become nothing but evil.

CHORUS

Loudly shall I send, to greet your return,° 935
an evil-omened shout, an evil-practiced cry:
a weeping wail I shall sing,
the wail of a Mariandynian mourner. 940

XERXES

ANTISTROPHE A

Send a wail of evil sound
lamenting and grievous; now
this god again has changed for me.

CHORUS

Mourning wail all-weeping shall I send,
in honor of the people's sufferings and sea-struck toils:° 945
again a wailing filled with tears I'll cry.

XERXES

STROPHE B

Ionian Ares triumphed,

protector of their ships,
their partisan in war,
reaping gloomy flats of sea
and demon-haunted shores.

950

CHORUS

Oh, oh!
Lament and learn it all.
Where are the others?
Where is your retinue, your comrades
like Pharandakas,
Sousas, Pelagon, and Agabatas,
Dotamas, Psammis, Sousiscanes
who went from Agbatana?—

955

960

XERXES

ANTISTROPHE B

I left them dead there;
they fell from the Tyrian ships on the shore of Salamis,
and so were gone, their corpses
pounding stubborn shores.

965

CHORUS

Oh, oh! But where is Pharnouchus
and brave Ariomardus?
Where is lord Seualces,
Or noble-born Lilaeus,
Memphis, Tharybis, and Masistres,
Artembares and Hystaechmes?
All these I ask you about.

970

XERXES

STROPHE C

Oh oh, woe!
All of them, after gazing
on ancient, hateful Athens,
at one stroke, ah, ah, wretchedly
gasp out their lives on the shore.

975

CHORUS

Did you leave that Persian there too,
your trusted universal eye
who made his count by myriads,°   980
Batanochus' favorite son . . .
. . . of Seisames, of Megabates,°
great Parthus and Oebares you left behind?
O woe, O woe, O miseries!   985
You tell of woes on woes for the Persians.

XERXES

ANTISTROPHE C

Oh oh, woe!
The magic wheel of longing
for my friends you turn, you tell me   990
hateful sorrows. Within my body
my heart cries, cries out.

CHORUS

And for others still we are longing:
the leader of ten thousand men
of Mardia, Xanthes, and Anchares,
and Diaixis and Arsames,   995
masters of horsemen;
and Dadakes and Lythimnas,
and Tolmus insatiable in battle.
I am shocked to see about the moving tents   1000
none of these now following.

XERXES

STROPHE D

Gone are the hunters of the pack.

CHORUS

Gone, alas, nameless.

XERXES

Oh oh, woe.

CHORUS

Woe, O gods
who brought these unexpected miseries!   1005
How fiercely gleams the eye of doom.

XERXES

Struck from our success by woes . . .°

CHORUS

We've been struck by new . . .

XERXES

. . . by new agonies.   1010

CHORUS

Woe, ah!
We met the Ionian sailors without success:
how luckless was the Persians' war.

XERXES

Ah, I am struck, appalled that I lost such an army.

CHORUS

What is not lost, you curse of the Persians?   1015

XERXES

Look at the remnants of my power.

CHORUS

I see, I see.

XERXES

And this receptacle . . .

CHORUS

What is this that is saved?

XERXES

. . . my treasure of arrows.   1020

CHORUS

How few from so many!

XERXES

We are deprived of protectors.

CHORUS

The Greeks stand firm in combat. 1025

XERXES

Alas, too firm! I saw an unexpected misery.

CHORUS

You mean the crowd of ships, routed and broken?

XERXES

I tore my garments at this calamity. 1030

CHORUS

Ah, O woe!

XERXES

And even more than woe.

CHORUS

Double and triple the woe.

XERXES

Painful to us, but to enemies joy.

CHORUS

And cut short was our power. 1035

XERXES

I am stripped of escorts.

CHORUS

Sea-dooms stripped us of our friends.

XERXES

STROPHE F

Weep, wet your cheeks for the pain, and come homeward.

CHORUS

Ah, ah, misery.

XERXES

Cry out antiphonal to me. 1040

CHORUS

A woesome gift in response to woe.

XERXES

Raising a cry, join together our songs.

XERXES AND CHORUS

O woe, woe, woe upon woe.

CHORUS

Hearing this calamity,
Oh! I am pierced. 1045

XERXES

ANTISTROPHE F
Sweep, sweep, sweep with the oar, and groan for my sake.

CHORUS

Ah, ah! Pain, pain!

XERXES

Cry out antiphonal to me.

CHORUS

My duty is here, O master, lord.

XERXES

Lift up your voice in lamenting now. 1050

XERXES AND CHORUS

O woe, woe, woe upon woe.

CHORUS

Black with bruises again the blows are mixed,
Oh, with the groans.

XERXES

STROPHE G

Beat your breast too and cry Mysian laments.

CHORUS

Pain, pain.   1055

XERXES

Tear the whitened hair of your beard.

CHORUS

With clenched hand, grimly mourning.

XERXES

Shriek a piercing cry.

CHORUS

And so I shall.

XERXES

ANTISTROPHE G

Tear the folds of your garments with strength of hand.   1060

CHORUS

Pain, pain.

XERXES

Pluck your hair and voice your pity for the army.

CHORUS

With clenched hand, grimly mourning.

XERXES

Drench your eyes.

CHORUS

Yes, so I weep.   1065

XERXES

EPODE

Cry out antiphonal to me.

CHORUS
Oh, O woe.

XERXES
Go wailing to your homes.

CHORUS
O woe, ah!

XERXES
Cries of woe throughout the city.   1070

CHORUS
Yes, cries of woe indeed.

XERXES
Softly stepping, moan in grief.

CHORUS
O Persian land in hardness stepped.°

XERXES
Oh, oh, by triple banks of oars . . .

CHORUS
Oh, oh, . . . our ships were destroyed by theirs.

CHORUS
We shall escort you
with mournful lament.

(Exit all.)

THE SEVEN AGAINST THEBES

Translated by DAVID GRENE

THE SEVEN AGAINST THEBES: INTRODUCTION

The Play: Date and Composition

Aeschylus' *Seven against Thebes* was first produced in 467 BCE, as the third play of a connected tetralogy consisting of *Laius*, *Oedipus*, *The Seven against Thebes*, and the satyr-drama *Sphinx*. Aeschylus won first prize that year in the competition. Second place went to Aristias with four plays actually composed by his father, Pratinas, who was a famous dramatist and one of Aeschylus' chief rivals; and third place went to Polyphrasmon, the son of another of Aeschylus' old rivals, Phrynichus, for a connected tetralogy about Lycurgus, a Thracian who resisted the cult of Dionysus rather as Pentheus did.

There are several references in our play to events and predictions from the first two plays of the tetralogy; and the plot of *The Seven against Thebes* itself constitutes the final phase of a long and drawn-out story, just as Aeschylus' *Eumenides* wraps up the whole *Oresteia*. Unfortunately, the ending of the play as we have it looks as if it has been modified from what Aeschylus wrote and presented in 467 BCE. Most modern scholars are convinced that the play was extensively rewritten in order to align it with the plotline of Sophocles' *Antigone* (which was first produced some fifteen years after Aeschylus' death). As a result, the ending in the surviving manuscripts appears to diverge significantly from the plot trajectory of Aeschylus' original play. This uncertainty about the ending makes our reconstruction of the rest of the trilogy all the more difficult and speculative. But for the most part *The Seven against Thebes*, the second-earliest of Aeschylus' surviving dramas, has a simple structure, and its action and meaning are relatively easy to follow.

The Myth

The story of the doomed descendants of King Labdacus of Thebes—Laius, Oedipus, and Oedipus' sons, Eteocles and Polynices—and of the tribulations endured by the city of Thebes as a result of this family's incest and murders was quite famous and often recounted in early Greek literature. For example, it figured in epic poems, now lost, attributed to Homer or one of his successors, and in many lyric poems, including one from the sixth-century poet Stesichorus of which fragments survive on papyrus. As with almost all Greek myths, there were many different versions and variations of the story, but the main outlines remain fairly consistent: King Laius and his wife, Jocasta (sometimes she is given a different name), are informed by the oracle of Apollo that they must not have a baby (it seems that in Aeschylus' version Laius was told that the safety of the city depended on his remaining childless). But they do proceed to have a baby son anyway, who grows up to be Oedipus. Their reason for flouting the oracle's warning is only hinted at in *The Seven against Thebes* (lines 750-57), though it may have been explained more fully in one of the earlier plays of the trilogy. In some versions, Jocasta got Laius drunk and then seduced him into having intercourse; in others, Laius' excessive sexual appetite led him astray. When the baby is born, it is taken out and abandoned to die. In Aeschylus' *Laius*, apparently the baby was placed in a pot when it was exposed, but we do not have any details of how his rescue and upbringing were managed (though it is quite likely that these details were different from Sophocles' version in *Oedipus the King*).

In due course, Oedipus encounters his real father at a crossroads, though neither recognizes the other. They fight and Oedipus kills Laius. He then comes to Thebes, which is being terrorized by the monstrous Sphinx. Oedipus solves the Sphinx's riddle and is hailed as the new king by the Thebans, which entails marrying the widow of the recently deceased ruler—no one knows that she is his mother. In most versions of the story Oedipus and Jocasta have four children: two boys, Polynices and

Eteocles, and two girls, Antigone and Ismene. Eventually, the truth about Oedipus' identity (and the parricide and incest) is discovered. What happens next varies from one version to another. In some accounts, Jocasta commits suicide; in others not. In some, Oedipus continues to be the king of Thebes; in others he goes into exile or is deposed from the throne but remains in Thebes. In some, he blinds himself: it is not known when or by whom this detail of self-blinding was invented (it is mentioned in *The Seven against Thebes*, lines 778–84).

The ghastly problems continue into the next generation, with Oedipus' two sons quarreling violently about the succession. (In some versions of the story, including Euripides' *Phoenician Women*, Oedipus is still alive throughout their dispute; in others, including Sophocles' *Oedipus at Colonus* and *Antigone*, as well as Aeschylus' *Seven against Thebes*, he has already died.) Again, different accounts exist of this quarrel and its consequences, though all include reference to Oedipus' laying a curse on his two sons. The curse, which in *The Seven against Thebes* is described as a "Fury," like the curses of Clytaemestra in the *Eumenides*, entails that the two brothers will never be able to divide their inheritance and the kingdom peacefully, but will end up killing one another. An arrangement is made between them: in some versions, they agree to alternate the rule annually, but Eteocles then refuses to relinquish the throne after his first year is over; in other versions, Polynices agrees to take a large share of movable property, while Eteocles becomes the permanent king of Thebes. We do not know how this issue was handled in Aeschylus' trilogy. But in all versions, Polynices leaves Thebes to live for a while in Argos. There he marries Argeia, the daughter of the Argive king, Adrastus, and Polynices persuades the Argives to provide him with an army, with the intention of gaining the Theban throne by force.

This is the point at which *The Seven against Thebes* begins. Polynices and six other champions from Argos (the "Seven against Thebes") are about to attack the city at its seven gates, while Eteocles is busy organizing the city's defense. As the messenger describes the opposing champions in turn, Eteocles dispatches six

Theban champions to match them, one at each gate, countering each of the enemies' boasts and shield emblems with the most appropriate opponent. He ends up selecting himself as the seventh champion—so that he will face his own brother Polynices at the seventh gate. In due course it is reported by a messenger that in the ensuing battle the two brothers have met face to face and have killed one another. Still, the Argive invaders are repelled and the city is not captured.

Most scholars believe this is where Aeschylus' play and trilogy properly end: the ruling dynasty of the Labdacids has been destroyed, but the city of Thebes has survived. It has been emphasized throughout that both brothers share an identical fate, just as their father had cursed them. If this is the original ending, then this drama would conclude, as many do, with choral lamentation over the bodies. But in the text of the play contained in our medieval manuscripts, the plot suddenly takes a new and unexpected turn near the end: Antigone and Ismene, Oedipus' two daughters—who have not been mentioned at all during earlier scenes—arrive on stage; a herald informs everyone that the new ruler, Creon (who has also not been previously mentioned), has issued an edict granting to one brother, Eteocles, an honorific civic burial while the other, Polynices, is to be left unburied for the animals and birds to devour. At this point Antigone announces that she will defy Creon's edict and go and bury Polynices herself, even at the risk of execution. There the play ends, with no further resolution of this new set of issues. Most modern scholars believe that this final scene is a later revision of Aeschylus' original play in order to align it with Sophocles, and that in his original trilogy Antigone and Ismene did not appear at all.

The Remains of the Trilogy and Tetralogy

Of the first two plays of the tragic trilogy, we possess only tiny scraps. From *Laius* there is a reference to the "pot" in which the newborn Oedipus was placed, and a grisly mention of a murderer who tasted and spat out his victim's blood. One of the plays appears to have contained a messenger speech in which the meeting of Laius and Oedipus was described. Three lines survive:

> We were traveling along the road, and came
> to a three-way junction of the wagon tracks,
> as we were passing by the meeting of roads at Potniae.

For the rest, we have to imagine the content of those plays from what we know of the myth and—especially—from clues provided by the third play. *The Seven against Thebes* contains several references to Oedipus' curse and also to a dream, both of which seem to have been delivered in riddling fashion. In particular, mention is made of a "Scythian stranger" and a "Chalyb" (referring to the remote Scythian tribe that was credited by the Greeks with first inventing ironworking), who will assist the two brothers in dividing up the land inherited from their father. The audience understands that this prediction, presumably mentioned also in the preceding play, refers to the iron—the swords—with which they will kill each other, and that their inheritance will consist simply of graves in the Theban earth. But the chorus arrives at this conclusion only after Eteocles has gone off to confront his brother at the seventh gate. As they sing about their new realization (720-91), they also mention the original oracle of Apollo to Laius and Jocasta, their disastrous disobedience, Oedipus' discovery of his parricide, his self-blinding, and his cursing of his sons. Thus the buildup that has occupied most of the play, toward Eteocles' decision to assign himself as seventh champion to face his own hated brother in battle, culminates in this moment of recognition that the third and final phase of this family's dreadful history is now coming to its destined close.

As for the fourth play, the satyr-drama *Sphinx*, we know nothing for certain about its plot and possess only two short fragments. Athenian vase paintings depicting the Sphinx engaging with a group of satyrs probably reflect Aeschylus' play, but do not allow us to reconstruct it in any detail.

The Seven against Thebes was apparently one of Aeschylus' best-known plays throughout the fifth century BCE. This play (and Sphinx too) is mentioned conspicuously in Aristophanes' Frogs, and Euripides borrowed extensively from it in his Phoenician Women. After that, Aeschylus' play seems to have been quickly and almost permanently eclipsed in antiquity by the popularity of Euripides' more action-packed version, as also, to a lesser extent, by Sophocles' plays on Oedipus and Antigone. Nor does it appear that performances of connected trilogies were staged in theaters after the fifth century; so The Seven against Thebes, presumably in its current, adapted form, was catalogued and read separately from Laius and Oedipus. Aeschylus' plays in general were less widely read in schools or for pleasure than the plays of Sophocles or (especially) Euripides; most of them gradually ceased to be copied at all and thus faded into oblivion. When the time came to make a selected edition of seven Aeschylean plays (in the Roman period, perhaps for school use), Seven against Thebes was included, but none of the other plays of its trilogy.

The play survived into the Byzantine and Renaissance era and along with The Persians and Prometheus Bound became one of the triad of Aeschylean plays that were copied frequently during the twelfth to fifteenth centuries. As a result, some of the manuscripts of the play contain quite extensive marginal comments (scholia). There is little sign, however, that any authors or visual artists between the time of Euripides and the nineteenth century were much influenced by The Seven against Thebes, even though many versions of the Oedipus story and the mutual killing of his sons continued to be told and depicted. It was only with the rise of German Romanticism, and the consequent resurgence of enthusiasm for Aeschylus' archaic style and more direct and simple dramaturgy, that The Seven against Thebes came back into its own and was recognized as an early masterpiece of Western drama. The play is not often performed, mainly because of its rather static quality, with pairs of long descriptive speeches and limited stage action. Yet *The Seven against Thebes* has come to be admired for presenting the earliest, almost archetypical, example of a "tragic choice" in which the hero contemplates grim alternatives before coming to accept, even embrace, his overdetermined commitment to the inevitable path to ruin. Critics have noted how Aeschylus' text seems to leave the nature of this choice ambiguous — that is, whether Eteocles' choice of Theban champions, including himself, has already been made, or is actually taking place during the extended discussion with the Messenger. Is it the hero, or the gods, who bring about the brothers' encounter at the seventh gate?

Few adaptations or productions of the play have been attempted outside of college campuses. Notable are the adaptation by Cuban playwright Antón Arrufat (1968), the production of Aeschylus' play in Modern Greek by Karolos Koun (1975), and the hip-hop adaptation by Will Power (*The Seven*, 2003; 2006 with choreography by Bill T. Jones). Aeschylus' play also doubtless had an influence on Akira Kurosawa's classic *Seven Samurai* and John Sturges' *The Magnificent Seven*.

THE SEVEN
AGAINST THEBES

Characters°   ETEOCLES, son of Oedipus, and now ruler
of Thebes
MESSENGER
CHORUS of Theban women
ANTIGONE, sister of Eteocles
ISMENE, sister of Eteocles
HERALD

Scene: Thebes. Statues of gods stand near the center of the orchestra.

*(Enter Eteocles with attendants from the side,
to confront a crowd of Thebans.)*

ETEOCLES

You citizens of Cadmus, there is need
for good and timely counsel from the one
who watches over the progress of the ship
and guides the rudder, his eye not drooped in sleep.
For if we win success, god is the cause,
but if—may it not chance so—there is disaster,   5
throughout the town, voiced by its citizens,
a multitudinous much-repeated prelude
cries on one name "Eteocles" with groans:
may Zeus the Protector keep this from the city
of Cadmus, proving faithful to his title.
    You all must help her now—both you who still   10
are short of your full manhood and you who
have bodies grown to greater bulk and strength—

each of you to such duties as befit you:
help the city, help the altars of your country's gods;
save their honors from destruction;   15
help your children, help Earth your mother.
She reared you, on her kindly surface, crawling
babies, welcomed all the trouble of your nurture,
reared you to live here and to carry a shield
in her defense, loyally, against such needs as this.   20
And up to this day god kindly has inclined
for us who have been held in siege so long:
the war, with gods' help, goes quite favorably.
But now the prophet, tending the oracular birds
with skill infallible, through ears and mind—   25
no need of fire—the master of these prophecies,
says the enemy frames a plot this night
for the greatest Achaean assault upon us.
All to the battlements, to the gates of the towers!   30
Haste, in full armor, man the breastworks:
stand on the scaffolding and at the exit gates
be firm, abide, your hearts confident:
fear not that mighty mob of foreigners.   35

(Exit crowd of Thebans, to the side.)

God will dispose all well.
I have sent scouts and spies upon that host,
who will not—well I know it—make the journey
vainly; and by their information
I shall be armed against enemy stratagems.

(Enter Messenger from the other side.)

MESSENGER
Eteocles, great lord of the Cadmeans,
I come bringing a clear word about the army   40
out there, and about the way things stand: myself
I have seen the things that I speak of.
There were seven men, fierce regiment commanders;
they cut bulls' throats into an iron-rimmed

shield, and with hands touched the bulls' blood,
taking their oaths by Ares and Enyo,
and by the bloodthirsty god of Terror,   45
either to smash and lay your city level
with the ground, sacked, or by their death to make
a bloody paste of this same soil of yours.
Remembrances of themselves for parents at home
their hands have hung upon Adrastus' chariot: 50
their tears ran down,
but never a word of pity was in their mouths.
Their spirits were hard as iron and ablaze
breathed courage: war looked through their lion eyes.

     You will not wait long for confirmation
of this my news; I left them casting lots
how each should lead his regiment against your gates.   55
In view of this, choose the best men within your city
and set them at the entrance gates—quickly,
for near already the armed host of Argives
comes in a cloud of dust, with flecks of white,   60
panted from horses' lungs, staining the ground.
You, like the skillful captain of a ship
barricade your town before the blast of Ares
strikes it in storm: we already hear the roar
of the armed land wave. Take quickest opportunity   65
for all these things and I for the rest
will keep my eye, a trusty day watcher.
Thanks to my clear reports you shall know whatever
happens outside the gates, and come to no harm.

                              (Exit Messenger, to the side.)

ETEOCLES
O Zeus and Earth and gods that guard the city,
and mighty curse, the fury of my father,   70
do not root out this city of mine, do not
give her to ruin and destruction, do not
give her to capture nor her homes and hearths.

This is a town that speaks with a Greek tongue.
City and land of the Cadmeans are free:
do not bind her in slavish yoke; be her protector.   75
I think I speak for everybody's good,
for a city prospering gives honor to the gods.

       (*Exit Eteocles to one side. Enter the Chorus from the other side.*)

CHORUS [*singing*]
  My worries are great and fearful: I cry aloud:°
  the army has left the camp and runs free.
  Look at this forward-rushing river, the great tide of horsemen!   80
  I see a cloud of dust, sky-high, and am convinced;
  a messenger clear and truthful, though voiceless.
  Trampling hoofs on the earth of my country,
  the sound approaches my ears.
  It floats, it roars   85
  like a resistless mountain waterfall.
  O gods, O goddesses, turn aside
  the trouble raised!
  Over the walls comes the noise;
  the army of the white shield springs forward,   90
  well equipped, hastening upon our city.
  Who will protect us? Who will be our champion,
  what god or goddess?
  Shall I kneel at the images of the gods?   95
  O Blessed Ones, throned in peace,
  it is time to cling to your images.
  Why delay and wail too much?
  Do you hear or do you not the rattle of shields?   100
  When, if not now, shall we hang
  robes and garlands on your statues, supplicating?
  I see the sound—the clatter of many spears!
  What will you do, Ares,
  ancient lord of this country,
  will you betray your own land?   105

O spirit of the golden helmet, look down upon us,
look down upon a city
which once you dearly loved.

STROPHE A

City-guarding gods of our land, come, come all of you,   110
look upon us, a band of virgins,
suppliants against slavery!
Around our city the wave of warriors, with waving plumes,
roars; blasts of the war god stir them.   115
Ah, Zeus, Father all-ruling, all-fulfilling,
protect us at all costs from capture by our foes!
For the Argives are encircling Cadmus' city;   120
fear of their warlike arms dismays us.°
There is murder in the clanging harnesses
and the bits between their horses' jaws.
Seven proud captains of the host,   125
with harness and spear,
have won their place by lot;
they stand champions at seven gates.

ANTISTROPHE A

O powerful battle-loving daughter of Zeus,
save our city, Pallas!   130
And the horse-loving ruler of the sea,°
king of the trident, Poseidon,
grant deliverance from fear, deliverance.   135
You, Ares, ah! Protect the city that bears Cadmus' name;
show your care for it, in manifest presence.
And Cypris, who are our ancestress,   140
turn destruction away. We are sprung from your blood
and we approach you and cry
with prayers for the ears of the gods.   145
And you, wolf god, be a very wolf
to the enemy host; and you, daughter of Leto,
make ready your bow.

Ah, ah,   150
the rattle of chariots round the city: I hear it.
O Lady Hera,
the groaning axles of the loaded wheels!
Beloved Artemis,
the air is mad with the whirr of spears!   155
What will happen to our city, what will become of it,
what is the end that the gods are bringing?

Ah, ah,
there comes a shower of stones on the top of the battlements!
O beloved Apollo!   160
There is the rattle of bronze-bound shields at our gates!
O son of Zeus
from whom comes war's fulfilment
in the battle's holy outcome!
O Athena, blessed queen, champion of the city,
protect your seven-gated home!   165

O gods all-sufficient,
O gods and goddesses, perfecters,
protectors of our country's forts,
do not betray this city, spear-won,
to a foreign-tongued enemy.   170
Hear O hear the prayers, hand outstretched,
of these maidens supplicating in justice.

O beloved spirits
that encompass our city to its deliverance,   175
show how much you love it:
bethink you of the public sacrifices,
as we have thought of you, rescue us.
Remember, I pray you, the rites   180
with loving sacrifice offered by this city.

(Enter Eteocles from the side.)

ETEOCLES
   You insupportable creatures, I ask you,
   is this the best, is this for the city's safety,
   is this enheartening for our beleaguered army,
   to have you falling at the images   185
   of the city's gods crying and howling,
   an object of hatred for all people with sense?
   Neither in evils nor in fair good fortune
   may I share a dwelling with the tribe of women!
   When she's triumphant, hers is confidence
   that others cannot deal with; when afraid,
   a greater evil both for home and city.   190
   So now, running wild among the citizenry
   you have shrieked them into spiritless cowardice,
   as outside our gates, the enemy gains strength
   while we, within, are by ourselves undone.
   All this you may have, for living with women!   195
       Now if there is anyone that will not hear
   my orders, be he man or woman or in between,
   sentence of death shall be decreed against him
   and public stoning he shall not escape.
   Affairs outside are a man's province: let no   200
   woman debate it: within doors, do no mischief!
   Do you hear me or not? Or are you deaf?

CHORUS [*singing in alternation with Eteocles, who speaks in response*]
STROPHE A
Dear son of Oedipus, the bumping rattle of the chariots,
rattle, rattle, I am afraid when I hear,
when the naves of the axles screech in their running,   205
when the fire-forged bits speak ringingly,
rudder oars in horses' mouths.

ETEOCLES
   What—shall the sailor, then, who leaves the stern

and runs to the prow find any device for safety
when his vessel is foundering in the sea waves? 210

CHORUS

But it was to the images of the gods,
the ancient images, I ran, trusting in the gods,
when the stony blizzard crashed upon our gates:
that was when I leaped up in fear and betook myself to prayer
to the Blessed Ones, for our city,
that they may make their strength its protection. 215

ETEOCLES

For protection pray that our towers hold off
the enemy's spears. That shall be as the gods dispose.°
But the gods, they say, of a captured town desert it.

CHORUS

STROPHE B

Never in my lifetime, never may this assembly
of gods desert us: never may I live to see 220
this city overrun, an enemy soldiery
putting the torch to it.

ETEOCLES

Do not call upon the gods and then take foolish counsel.
Obedience is mother to success,
and wife of salvation—so runs the proverb. 225

CHORUS

ANTISTROPHE B

This is true, but the strength of god is still greater.
Oftentimes when someone is hopelessly sunk
in misfortune, a god raises him, even from the greatest trials
with the clouds hanging high above his eyes.

ETEOCLES

But it is men's part, the sacrifice, the consultation 230

of the gods, when the enemy assaults us;
it is yours to be silent and stay within doors.

CHORUS

STROPHE C

It is thanks to the gods that we have our city
unconquered; it is thanks to them
that our towers reject the mob of foemen.
What should be resented in these words?   235

ETEOCLES

I do not grudge your honoring the gods.
But lest you turn our citizens into cowards,
be quiet and not overfearful.

CHORUS

ANTISTROPHE C

It was but now that I heard the noise
and the confusion, so that trembling
in fear I came to this citadel,   240
this honored and sacred seat.

ETEOCLES

If you shall learn of men dying or wounded,
do not be eager to anticipate it with cries,
for slaughtered men are Ares' favorite food.

CHORUS LEADER [*now speaking*]

The snorting of horses! There, I hear it.   245

ETEOCLES

Do not listen; do not hear too much.

CHORUS LEADER

Our city groans from its foundation: we're surrounded.

ETEOCLES

It's sufficient for me to think of this, not you.

CHORUS LEADER

I am afraid: the din at the gates grows louder.

ETEOCLES

Silence! Do not speak of this throughout the city. 250

CHORUS LEADER

O blessed assembly, do not betray this fort.

ETEOCLES

Damnation! Can you not endure in silence?

CHORUS LEADER

Fellow-citizen gods, grant me not to be a slave.

ETEOCLES

You're enslaving yourselves, and me, and all the city.

CHORUS LEADER

O Zeus, all-mighty, your bolt upon our foes! 255

ETEOCLES

O Zeus, what a tribe you have given us in women!

CHORUS LEADER

Useless too are men, when their town's been captured.

ETEOCLES

These are ill-omened words, when your hands are on the
images!

CHORUS LEADER

Fear captures my tongue, and my spirit is quite gone.

ETEOCLES

Grant me, I pray you, the small thing I ask. 260

CHORUS LEADER

Speak it quickly, that I may know at once.

ETEOCLES

Silence, you wretches, don't frighten your friends.

CHORUS LEADER

I am silent; with others I'll endure what is fated.

ETEOCLES

I like this word better than those before.
Furthermore, get you away from the statues, 265
and being so, utter a better prayer:
"May the gods stand as our allies." So first hear
my prayer and then offer your own—
a holy gracious paean of victory,
the cry of sacrifice, as is Greek custom,
joy to our friends, dissolving fear of foes. 270
Gods of the city and community,
lords of its fields and its assembly places;
springs of Dirce, waters of Ismenus—
to you my vow:
if all go well with us, if the city is saved,
my people shall redden your hearths with the blood 275
of sacrificed sheep, and with the blood
of bulls slaughtered to honor the gods.°
I shall myself dedicate trophies,
spoils of my enemies, their garments fixed
on spear points, in your sanctuaries.

(To the Chorus.)

These be your prayers, unlamenting
with no vain wild panting and moaning: 280
for none of that will bring escape from destiny.
I will take six men, myself to make a seventh,
and go to post them at the city's gates,
opponents of the enemy, in gallant style,°
before quick messengers are on us and 285
their words of haste burn us with urgency.

(Exit Eteocles to the side.)

CHORUS [singing]
STROPHE A
I heed him, but through fear
my spirit knows no sleep;

and neighbors to my heart,
anxieties kindle terror
of the host that beleaguers us,   290
as the all-fearing dove
dreads for its nestlings' sake
the snakes that menace them.
For some of them advance against our walls   295
with full armor and full ranks—
what will become of me?—
while others hurl jagged rocks   300
upon our citizens. O gods of Zeus's family,
I pray you—protect on every front
the city and the army,
the Cadmus-born!

What country will you take in exchange,
better than this one,   305
if you abandon this deep-soiled land
to her enemies,
and Dirce's water, fairest to drink
of all that come from Poseidon
the earth-upholder, and Tethys' sons?   310
Therefore, you city-guarding gods,
upon the men outside our forts
rain slaughtering destruction
and ruin that will cast away their shields: 315
and for these citizens here
win glory and of the city
be the rescuers.
Stand fair in your places
to receive our shrill prayers.   320

Pitiful it would be for this city, so ancient,
to be cast to the House of Death,
a spear-booty, a slave,

in crumbling ashes, shamefully
sacked by an Achaean man, with the gods' consent;   325
that its women be dragged away, ah!
captives, young and old,
dragged by the hair, as horses by the mane,
and their clothing torn about them.
The city wails as it's emptied out   330
and the captive spoil with mingled cries
is led to its doom.
This heavy fate is what I fear.

ANTISTROPHE B

Woeful is it for maidens new-reared and unripe,
before the marriage rites, to tread
this bitter journey from their homes.   335
I would say that even the dead
are better off than this.
Ah, unlucky indeed the fate
of a city captured—
here, there, everywhere
murder, fire, and rapine,   340
all the city polluted by smoke,
and the breath of Ares on it
maddened, desecrating piety, slaying the people.

STROPHE C

There is tumult through the town.   345
All around it hangs a towering net:
man stands against man with the spear and is killed.
Screams, bloody and wild, echo around,
from babies new-nourished at the breast.   350
The roving bands of pillagers are all brothers;
he that has plunder meets with another;
he that has none calls him that has none,
wishing to have a partner, eager for a share
neither less nor yet equal.   355
From such things what shall one predict?°

All sorts of grain fallen,
strewn on the ground, pain
the eye, with fierce new owners.°
The great, profuse gifts of the earth   360
in reckless streams of waste are poured out.
The girls, new servants, new to misery,
must endure a war captive's bed,
the bed of a successful man.   365
Theirs the expectation of night's consummation
with the triumphant enemy,
as help for their tearful sorrows.

(Enter the Messenger, from one side.)

FIRST HALF-CHORUS [*speaking*]
  Here, I think, friends, our scout comes bringing
  some news of the enemy—hastily urging   370
  the joints of his legs to carry him here.

(Enter Eteocles, from the other side.)

SECOND HALF-CHORUS [*speaking*]
  And here is the king himself, the son
  of Oedipus, in the nick of time to hear
  the messenger's story. He too is in haste
  and nimbly steps along.

MESSENGER
              I can declare—
  I know it well—the enemy's position: 375
  how each at the gates has won by lot his station.
  At the Proetid gate Tydeus now thunders
  but dares not cross Ismenus' ford; the prophet
  forbids. The sacrifices are unfavorable.
  Tydeus, enraged and thirsting for the fight,   380
  threatens, like serpents' hiss at noonday;
  he strikes with abuse the wise seer, son of Oecles.

"Battle and death make him cringe
through cowardice"—so he shouts aloud
and shakes his threefold shadowing plumes,   385
the mane of his crested helm. Beneath his shield,
inside, ring brazen bells, a peal of terror,
and on the shield he bears this arrogant
device—a fashioned sky afire with stars.
In the shield's midst a glorious full moon,
night's eye, the eldest of the stars, stands out.   390
With such mad bragging and with overweening
trappings of war he roars along the banks
in love with battle, like the horse that chafes
against the bit, high-mettled, impatient, hearing
the trumpet's sound. Against this champion
whom will you set?
When the bolts are shot back at the Proetid gates,   395
who will be champion fit to deserve our trust?

ETEOCLES

No equipment of a man will make me tremble.
Devices on a shield deal no one wounds.
The plumes and bells bite not without the spear.
And for this night you speak of on his shield   400
glistening with all the stars of heaven—someone
may find his folly prophetic to himself.
For if in death night fall upon his eyes,
to him that bears this pompous blazonry
it shall be truly and most justly eloquent,   405
and he shall make his insolence prophesy
against himself.
                    I nominate against him
as champion of these gates to challenge Tydeus,
the worthy son of Astacus—right noble,
one honoring the throne of Modesty
and hating insolent words.   410
He's not a doer of anything shameful; and his way

is never a coward's. From those Sown Men
whom Ares spared his root is sprung—quite native
is Melanippus to this land. The outcome
shall Ares with his dice determine; but
Justice, blood of his blood, now sends him forth,
surely, to turn the enemy's spear away   415
from the mother that has borne him, his homeland.

CHORUS [*singing*]

STROPHE A

May the gods grant
good luck to our champion,
since justly he comes forward,
a fighter for our city.
But I fear to look
upon the bloody ends of those dying   420
on behalf of those they love.

MESSENGER

Yes, may the gods grant him good luck.
At Electra's gates stands by lot Capaneus,
a giant this man, taller than the other,
and his threats breathe inhuman arrogance.   425
Our towers he menaces with terrors—Fortune
fulfill them not!°—for he declares he'll sack
our city with gods' favor or without it:
not even Zeus's weapon striking the earth
shall be obstacle to his purpose. The lightning
flashes and the thunderbolts he likened   430
to the sun's warm rays at noontide.
                                    The device
he bears—a naked man that carries fire,
in his hands, ablaze, a torch all ready. In gold
are letters that declare "I'll burn the city."
Against this man send—who will meet him?   435
Who will await his threats and never tremble?

ETEOCLES

This man's boasts, too, beget us other gain.
For of the arrogance of vain men, the true
accuser is their own tongue. Capaneus
threatens to act—and is prepared to act— 440
in contempt of the gods; and giving exercise
to his mouth, in vain joy, up to heaven
mortal though he is, against Zeus sends his words,
shouted in swelling pride. I trust that to him
will justly come the bolt that carries fire 445
in no way like the sun's warm rays at noontide.
Against him, be his lips ever so insolent,
a man of fiery spirit has been stationed,
strong Polyphontes, a guardian trustworthy,
by favor of protecting Artemis 450
and of the other gods. Tell me another
that has his place by lot at another gate.

CHORUS [*singing*]

ANTISTROPHE A

Destruction on him that against the city
vaunts huge threats;
may the thunderbolt's blast restrain him
before he bursts into my house, 455
before he ravishes me from my maiden room.

MESSENGER

Now I shall speak of him that by lot won
next station at the gates. The third lot cast
jumped from the upturned brazen helmet
in favor of a third man, Eteoclus,
that he should lead his regiment in a charge 460
against the gates of Neïs. He wheels his mares
snorting in their nose bands, ready to charge the gate.
Pipes on the bridle bands filled with insolent
nostril breath whistle in a foreign note.

His shield, too, has its design—and not a small one—   465
a man in armor mounts a ladder's steps
to the enemy's town to sack it. Loud
cries also this man in his written legend,
"Ares himself shall not cast me from the tower."
Against him send some champion trustworthy   470
to turn the yoke of slavery from this city.

ETEOCLES

He's already sent—and may good luck go with him!
His boast is in his hands: he's Megareus,
Creon's son, and of the seed and race
of the Sown Men. He will never blench
at the furious neighing of horses nor yield the gates.   475
Either by death he'll pay his nurture's due
to his own land or he will capture two men
and city as depicted on the shield
and crown his father's house with the spoils of war.
On with another's boasts—don't begrudge me the story.   480

CHORUS [*singing*]

Good success to you, I pray,
O champion of my house,
and to the enemy ill success!
As with wild extravagance
they boast loudly against the city
with maddened heart, so may Zeus
the punisher look on them in wrath.   485

MESSENGER

Another, the fourth, holds the gate that neighbors
Onca Athena, and takes his station with a shout,
Hippomedon's vast frame and giant form.
He whirled a disc around—I mean the circle
of his shield—until I shuddered. I speak truth.   490
The armorer cannot have been a poor one
that put upon the shield this work of art—

Typhon hurling from his fiery mouth
black smoke, the flickering sister of fire;
and the rim that ran around the hollow boss
of the shield is solid wrought with coiling snakes.   495
The man himself cried out his warcry: he,
inspired by Ares, revels in violence
like a Bacchanal with murder in his glance.
Take good heed how you deal with such a man;
he boasts even now at the gate he will raise panic.   500

ETEOCLES
First, Onca Pallas, with her place beside
our city, neighbor to our gates, will hate
the fellow's violence and keep him off,
as it were a chill snake from her nestling brood.
And then Hyperbius, the stout son of Oenops,
has been chosen to match him man for man, right willing,   505
at fortune's need, to put his fate to question—
a man not to be reproached either in form
or spirit or in bearing of his arms.
Hermes has matched the two with excellent reason,
for man with man they shall engage as foes
and on their shields shall carry enemy gods.   510
The one has Typhon breathing fire, the other,
Hyperbius, has father Zeus in station
sitting upon his shield, and in his hand
a burning bolt.
No one has ever yet seen Zeus defeated.°
Such on each side are the favors of the gods;   515
we are on the winning side, they with the vanquished
if Zeus is truly mightier in war than Typhon.
According to the logic of the emblems,
Zeus on Hyperbius' shield should be our savior.   520

CHORUS [*singing*]
ANTISTROPHE B
My faith is strong that the one who has

Zeus's adversary on his shield,
the unloved form of the earth-born demon,
an image hated by men
and by the long-living gods,
shall lose his head before our gates. 525

MESSENGER
So may it prove. Now I speak of the fifth
that is stationed at the fifth, the Northern gate,
right by Amphion's tomb that sprung from Zeus.
By his spear he swears—and with sure confidence
he holds it more in reverence than a god, 530
more precious than his eyes—he will sack the town
of Thebes in despite of Zeus. Such the loud vaunt
of this creature sprung of a mountain mother, handsome,
something between a man and a young boy.
The beard is newly sprouting on his cheeks,
the thick, upspringing hair of youth in its bloom. 535
His spirit unlike his maiden name is savage,
and with a Gorgon look he now advances.
He too boasts high as he draws near our gates:
for on his brazen shield, his body's rounded
defense, he swings an insult to our city, 540
the Sphinx that ate men raw, cunningly wrought,
burnished, embossed, secured with rivets there;
a man she bears beneath her, a Cadmean,
so that at him most of our shafts shall fly.
When he comes to the battle, so it seems,
he will not play the petty shopkeeper 545
of war nor shame his lengthy journey here—
Parthenopaeus of Arcadia.
He lives among our enemy presently
and pays to Argos a fair wage for his keep,
with threats against our walls—may god not grant them!

ETEOCLES
May they themselves obtain what from the gods 550

they pray against us—they, and their impious boasts!
Then would they perish utterly and ill.
We have a man to encounter your Arcadian,
a man unboasting but his hand looks for
the thing that should be done—Actor, the brother 555
of him I spoke of earlier. He will not allow
a heedless tongue to flow within our gates
and to breed mischief, nor to cross our walls
one bearing on his enemy shield the likeness
of that most hateful Sphinx. And when the beast
is hammered hard and beaten outside our walls
she'll blame the man who tried to carry her in. 560
With the gods' will, what I say will turn out true.

CHORUS [*singing*]

STROPHE C

The words go through my heart;
the hair stands upright on my head;
as I listen to mighty words 565
of impious boasting men.
If gods are gods, may they destroy them within our land!

MESSENGER

A sixth I'll tell you of—a most modest man
greatest in might of battle, yet a prophet:
strong Amphiaraus at the Homoloian gates 570
is stationed, shouting insults at strong Tydeus:
"Murderer, wrecker of your city, greatest
teacher of evil to Argos; of the Fury
a summoning herald; servant of bloodshed;
adviser to Adrastus of all these evils." 575
And then again with eyes uplifted calling
on your own brother, strong prince Polynices,
he dwells twice on the last part of his name,
"the one of much strife."°
And this is the speech to which his lips give utterance:
"Is such a deed as this dear to the gods, 580

and fair to hear and tell of for posterity,
for one to sack his native town, destroy
the gods of his own country, bringing in
an alien enemy host? What claim of justice
shall quench the guilt that wells up from your mother,°
and your fatherland destroyed by the spear   585
which your own zeal impelled—shall it be your ally?
But for myself I shall make fat this soil
a prophet buried under enemy ground.
Let us fight. The fate I look for is right honorable."
So spoke the prophet brandishing his round°   590
brazen shield. No device is on its circle.
He is best not at seeming to be such
but being so. Deep indeed is the furrow
of his mind from which he gathers fruit, and good
the counsels that do spring from it. For him
send out, I recommend, wise and good challengers,   595
for he is dangerous who reveres the gods.

ETEOCLES
Alas, the luck which among human beings
can join an honest man with impious ones!
In every enterprise is no greater evil
than bad companionship: there is no fruit   600
worth gathering from it. The field of doom
bears death as its harvest.
Indeed, a pious man, going on board
as shipmate of a crew of criminals
and of some mischief they have perpetrated,
has often died with the god-detested breed;
or a just man, with fellow citizens   605
themselves inhospitable, forgetful of the gods,
has fallen into the same snare as the unrighteous,
and smitten by the common scourge of god
has yielded up his life.
                    Even so this seer,

this son of Oecles, wise, just, good, and holy,   610
a prophet mighty, mingling with the impious—
against his better reason—with loud-mouthed
men who pursue a road long to retrace,
with Zeus's will shall be dragged to collective doom.
I think he will not even assault the gate—   615
not that he is a coward or faint of spirit—
but well he knows how he must die in the battle
if Loxias' prophecies shall bear fruit
(and either the god says nothing, or speaks what's true).
Yet still, against him, the mighty Lasthenes   620
we shall post in combat, an inhospitable
sentry, in mind an old man but a young one
in his body's vigor, in his swift-flying gaze,
and in his hand, not slow to take his spear
and drive it where the shield reveals a chink.
But success—for men that's the gift of god alone.   625

CHORUS [*singing*]

ANTISTROPHE C

Hear, O gods, our righteous prayers
and bring them to fulfilment, that
the city prosper, diverting
the horrors of war onto our invaders.
May Zeus strike them and slay them
with his bolt outside our walls.   630

MESSENGER

And now, the seventh at the seventh gate
I shall unfold—your own, your very brother.
Hear how he curses the city and what fate
he invokes upon her. He prays that once his foot
is set upon our walls, once he is proclaimed
the conqueror of this land, once he has cried
a paean of triumph in its overthrow,°   635
he then may close in fight with you and killing
encounter his own death beside your corpse.

Or if you live, that he may banish you—
in the selfsame way as you dishonored him—
to exile. So he shouts and calls the gods
of his race and of his fatherland to witness 640
his prayers—a very violent Polynices.
He bears a new-made, rounded shield, and on it
a twofold device, skillfully contrived:
a woman leading modestly a man
pictured as a warrior, wrought all in gold.
She guides him, and she claims that she is Justice; 645
and the inscription reads: I will bring him home,
and he shall have his city and shall walk
in his ancestral house.
                    Such are the signs.
But you yourself determine whom to send. 650
You shall not find a fault in my report:
but you determine how to steer the state.

ETEOCLES
Our family, the family of Oedipus,
by the gods maddened, by them greatly hated;
ah, my father's curses are now fulfilled! 655
But from me no crying and no lamentation,
lest grief arise yet harder to endure.
I can say about Polynices, so well named,
soon we shall know the pertinence of his sign,
whether his golden characters on the shield, 660
babbling, in wild distraction of the mind,
will indeed bring him home. This might have been,
if Justice, Zeus's virgin daughter, had stood
by his actions and his mind. But in his flight
out of the darkness of his mother's womb,
in his growth as a child, in his young manhood, 665
in the first gathering of his beard—no, never
did Justice look upon him nor regard him.
I do not think that now, as he comes to outrage

this fatherland of his, she will stand his ally—
or else she is falsely called Justice, joining 670
with a man whose mind conceives no limit in villainy.
In this I trust, and to the conflict with him
I'll go myself. What other has more right?
King against king, and brother against brother,
foe against foe we'll fight. 675
           Bring me my greaves
to shield me from the lances and the stones.

CHORUS LEADER
O dearest son of Oedipus, do not
be like in temper to this dire speaker
of dreadful sayings. There are enough Cadmeans
to grapple with the Argives: such blood is expiable. 680
But for the blood of brothers mutually shed
there is no growing old of the pollution.

ETEOCLES
If a man suffer ill, let it be without shame;
this is the only gain when we are dead.
But for deeds both evil and disgraceful, never 685
will you speak a word of glory or of good.

CHORUS [singing]

STROPHE A

What do you long for, child?
Let not the frantic lust
for battle, filling the heart,
carry you away. Expel
the evil passion at its birth.

ETEOCLES [speaking]
It is the god that drives this matter on. 690
Since it is so—on, on with favoring wind
this wave of hell that has engulfed for its share
all kin of Laius, whom Phoebus has so hated!

CHORUS

ANTISTROPHE A

Bitter-biting indeed
is the passion that urges you
to accomplish manslaying,
bitter in fruit,
where the blood to be shed is unlawful.

ETEOCLES

Yes, for the hateful black
curse of my beloved father   695
sits with dry and tearless eyes
and tells me first of gain and then of death.

CHORUS

STROPHE B

Resist its urging: coward   700
you shall not be called
if you rule your life well.
Out from your house the black-robed Fury
shall go, when from your hands
the gods shall receive a sacrifice.

ETEOCLES

We are already past the care of gods.
For them our death is the delightful offering.°
Why then delay, cringing at final destruction?

CHORUS

ANTISTROPHE B

Not when the chance is yours—
for in the veering change   705
of spirit though late
perhaps the god may change
and come with kinder breath.
Now his blast is full.

ETEOCLES

Yes, Oedipus's curses have fanned that blast.

Too true the vision of sleepy nightmares   710
showing division of my father's heritage.

CHORUS LEADER

Listen to women, though you like it not.

ETEOCLES

Speak then of what may be. But keep it short.

CHORUS LEADER

Don't go yourself on this path to the seventh gate.

ETEOCLES

No words of yours will blunt my whetted purpose.   715

CHORUS

Yet even bad victory the gods hold in honor.

ETEOCLES

No soldier should endure to hear such words.

CHORUS

Do you wish to reap as harvest a brother's blood?

ETEOCLES

If gods give ill, no man may escape their giving.

(Exit Eteocles to the side.)

CHORUS [*singing*]

STROPHE A

I shudder at the goddess,   720
unlike all other gods,
who compasses destruction of the house,
utterly unforgetting, prophet of ill,
the Fury invoked by a father's curse.
I dread that it bring to pass
the furious invocations
of Oedipus astray in his mind.   725
This strife, death to his sons, spurs it on.

A stranger grants them land allotment,
a Chalyb, Scythian colonist,
a bitter divider of possessions—
fierce-hearted Iron. 730
Yes, he has allotted them land to dwell in,
as much as the dead may possess:
no share theirs of the broad plains.

When they die with mutual hand
mutually slaughtering
and earth's dust drinks 735
black clotted murder-blood,
who shall then give purification,
who shall wash away the stain?
O new evils of the house, 740
new mingled with the old!

Old is the transgression I tell
but swift in retribution:
to the third generation it abides. 745
Three times in Pythian prophecies
given at the navel-of-earth
Apollo had directed
King Laius to die without child
and save his city so . . .

. . . but he was mastered by loving folly 750
and begot for himself a doom,
father-killing Oedipus,
who sowed his mother's sacred soil,
whence he had sprung himself,
and endured a bloody root crop. 755
Madness was the coupler
of the crazed bridal pair.

Now, as it were, a sea
drives on the waves of trouble:
one sinks, another rises,
triple-crested around the hull 760
of the city, and breaks in foam.
Our defense between is but a little thing
no bigger than a wall in width.
I fear that with our princes
our city may be subdued. 765

STROPHE D

For heavy is the settlement
of ancient curses, to fulfilment brought.
The destructive evils don't pass away.
Prosperity, grown fat for thriving men,
requires the jettisoning 770
of all goods, utterly.

ANTISTROPHE D

What man has earned such admiration
of gods and men that shared his city
and of the general throng of mortals,
as Oedipus—who ever had such honor 775
as he that from his land had banished
the man-snatching Sphinx?

STROPHE E

But then, when first he realized
the meaning of his dreadful marriage,
distraught with pain and maddened in heart 780
he brought a double harm to fulfilment.
With patricidal hand
he reft himself of eyes
that dearer to him were than his own children.°

And on those children savage   785
maledictions he launched, ah!
for their cruel care of him
and wished they might divide
with iron-wielding hand his own possessions.
And now I fear   790
that the nimble-footed Fury is bringing those wishes to fulfilment.

                              (Enter Messenger from the side.)

MESSENGER

Take heart, daughters of Cadmus' land°: this city
has escaped the yoke of slavery. Fallen
are the vauntings of those monstrous men.
Our city's in smooth water now; though buffeted   795
by many assaults of the waves, it shipped no sea.
Our wall still stands protecting us, our gates
we barricaded with trustworthy champions.
For the most part all is well—at six of the gates.
The seventh the lord Apollo, Captain of Sevens,   800
took for himself: on Oedipus' offspring
he has fulfilled the ancient follies of Laius.

CHORUS LEADER

What new and awful thing concerns the city?°

MESSENGER

The men have died, killed by each other's hands.   805

CHORUS LEADER

Who? What do you mean? I'm terrified at your words.

MESSENGER

Get your wits and hear. Oedipus' two sons ...

CHORUS LEADER

Ah, ah, the evils that I prophesied!

MESSENGER

In very truth, crushed to the ground.

CHORUS LEADER

They both lie there? Bitter though it be, yet speak. 810

MESSENGER

With brothers' hands they achieved their mutual murder.
The city is saved, but of the royal pair
the ground has drunk the blood shed each by each.
So all too equal was their guiding spirit,°
and surely he has destroyed this hapless family. 815
　　　　So here is store of sorrow and joy at once.
The city has good fortune, but its lords,
the two generals, have divided the possessions
with hammered iron of Scythia. They shall have
what land suffices for a grave, swept there 820
down the wind of their father's ill-fated curses.

(Exit Messenger.)

CHORUS [*chanting*]°
[*O great Zeus and spirits that guard*
the city, you protectors
that guard our walls:
shall I rejoice, shall I cry aloud 825
for our city's safety?
or for those wretched ones, luckless and childless,
our generals, shall I lament?
They have earned their name too well
and "men of strife" they have perished 830
through impious intent.]

[*singing*]

STROPHE A

O black curse consummated
on the race, the curse of Oedipus!
An evil chill assails my heart.

I raise the dirge at the tomb 835
like a maenad, hearing
of their blood-dripping corpses,
of their ill-fated death.
Ill-omened indeed
is this melody of the spear.

ANTISTROPHE A

It has worked to an end, not failed, 840
the curse called on them by their father of old.
The decisions of Laius, wanting in faith,
have had effect till now.
My heart is troubled for the city;
divine warnings are not blunted.
O full of sorrows, this you have done, 845
a deed beyond belief.
Woes worthy of groaning
have come in very truth.

(Enter attendants, carrying the bodies of Eteocles and Polynices.)°

MESODE A

Here is visible evidence of the messenger's tale.
Twofold our griefs and double
the ills these two men wrought; 850
double the fated sorrow
now brought to fulfilment.
What shall I say, but that
here sorrows abide at the hearth of the house?°
　　But rowing in lamentation, friends,
as the winds of woe keep blowing,
beat your head with rhythmic hands 855
and ply the speeding stroke which sends
forth across Acheron, over and over,
the black-sailed ship, untrodden by Apollo and sunless,
on its mission
to the unseen shore that welcomes all. 860

[chanting]°
[Here they come to their bitter task,
Ismene and Antigone,
to make the dirge for their brothers.
With true sincerity, I think,
from their deep bosoms,   865
they shall utter a song of grief that fits the cause.
Us it concerns to sing,
before their song,
the ill-sounding Furies' dirge,
and the hateful Hades paean.
O most luckless in your brothers   870
of all women that fasten the girdle about their robes,
I cry, I groan: there is no guile
in my heart to check my true dirge.]

FIRST HALF-CHORUS°

                        STROPHE B

O misguided ones,   875
faithless to friends, unwearied in evil,
who plundered your father's house
to your misery, with the spear.

SECOND HALF-CHORUS
Wretched indeed, who found wretched deaths
to the ruin of your house.

FIRST HALF-CHORUS

                        ANTISTROPHE B

O you that tore the roof   880
from your house, you that glimpsed
monarchy in bitter rivalry, now
at last you are reconciled—by the sword.   885

SECOND HALF-CHORUS
Too truly has that dread spirit,
the Fury of Oedipus,
brought all this to fulfilment.

FIRST HALF-CHORUS

STROPHE C

Stricken through their left sides,
stricken indeed,
through ribs born from a common womb.   890
Ah, strange ones,
alas for the curse
of death that answered death!

SECOND HALF-CHORUS

A straight thrust to house and body   895
delivered by unspeakable wrath,
by the doom invoked by a father's curse,
which they shared without discord.

FIRST HALF-CHORUS

ANTISTROPHE C

Through the city the sound of groaning;   900
the walls groan aloud;
the plain that loved them groans.
There remain for their descendants
the possessions for which
their bitter fate was paid,
for which their strife arose,
for which they found the end of death.   905

SECOND HALF-CHORUS

With bitterness of heart they shared
their possessions in equality:
but to their loved ones not without blame
is their arbitrator,
nor does Ares receive thanks.   910

FIRST HALF-CHORUS

STROPHE D

By the stroke of the sword they are as they are.
By the stroke of the sword there awaits them—what?
Equal shares in their ancestral tomb, says someone.

SECOND HALF-CHORUS

A shrill cry escorts them from their house,   915
a cry heartrending,
a cry for its own griefs, its own woes,
in anguish of mind with no thought of joy,
weeping tears from a heart that breaks,   920
for these our two princes.

FIRST HALF-CHORUS

ANTISTROPHE D

One may say over the bodies
of this unhappy pair:
much have they done to their fellow citizens,
and much to all the ranks of foreigners
who died in this devastating war.   925

SECOND HALF-CHORUS

Unlucky she that bore them
above all womankind
that are called by a mother's name.
She took as husband her own child
and bore these who have died,   930
their brotherly hands working each other's murder.

FIRST HALF-CHORUS

STROPHE E

Brotherly indeed in utter destruction,
in unkindly severance,
in frantic strife,   935
in the ending of their quarrel.

SECOND HALF-CHORUS

Their enmity is ended, in the earth
blood-drenched their life is mingled.
Very brothers are they now.   940
Bitter the reconciler of their feud,
stranger from over the sea,
sped hither by the fire,

whetted iron.
And a bitter, evil divider of possessions,
Ares, who made their father's curse 945
a thing of utter truth.

FIRST HALF-CHORUS

They have their share, unhappy ones,
of Zeus-given sorrows:
beneath their bodies, earth
in fathomless wealth shall lie. 950

SECOND HALF-CHORUS

You who have made your race
blossom with many woes:
over you at last the curses
have cried their shrill lament, 955
and the race is turned to confusion and rout.
The trophy of destruction stands
at the gates where they were smitten,
and conqueror of the two,
the haunting spirit at last has come to rest. 960

MESODE B [*the two Half-Choruses singing in alternation*]
—You smote and were smitten . . .
                    —you killed and were slain.
—By the spear you killed . . .
                    —by the spear you died.
—Wretched in acting . . .
                    —wretched in suffering.
—Let the groans go forth . . .
                    —let the tears fall.
—You lie in death . . .
                    —having killed. 965

STROPHE F
—Woe!

—Woe!
—My mind is maddened with groans . . .
        —with groans my heart is full.
Ah, ah, creature of tears . . .
        —you too, all-miserable!   970
By hand of kin you died . . .
        —and you killed one next of kin.
—A double sorrow to relate . . .
        —a double sorrow to see.
—Two sorrows hard by one another . . .
        —brother's sorrow close to brother's.

CHORUS [*singing in unison*]
O wretched Fate, giver of heavy grief,   975
awful shade of Oedipus,
black Fury,
truly you are a spirit mighty in strength!

        ANTISTROPHE F
—Woe!
        —Woe!
—Evils unfit to look upon . . .
        —he showed us after banishment.
—He came not back when he had slain . . .   980
        —This one came and lost his own life.
—This one died . . .
        —and killed the other.
—Unhappy family!
        —Unhappy deeds!
—Grievous sorrows of kindred . . .
        —Grievous, thrice grievous sorrow.   985

CHORUS [*in unison*]
O wretched Fate, giver of heavy grief,
awful shade of Oedipus,
black Fury,
truly you are a spirit mighty in strength.

—*You have learned the lesson by experience.*

         —*And you too have learned it, no whit later.*   990

—*When you returned to the city . . .*

         —*yes, to face him with your spear.*

—*Deadly to tell . . .*

         —*deadly to see.*

—*Pain . . .*

         —*ill . . .*

—*to house and land . . .*

         —*and most of all to me.*   995

—*O king, of grievous sorrows!*

         —*O of all most rich in pain!*   1000

—*O brothers possessed by evil spirits, in doom . . .*

         —*oh, where shall we lay them in the earth?*

—*Oh, where their honor shall be greatest.*

         —*Oh, sleeping by the side of their father to his hurt.*

         (Enter a Herald from the side.)°

HERALD

    It is my duty to declare to you,   1005
    counselors of the people, the resolves
    already taken and the present pleasure
    of this Cadmean city.

                Our lord Eteocles for his loyalty
    it is determined to bury in the earth
    that he so loved. Fighting its enemies
    he found his death here. In the sight
    of his ancestral shrines he is pure and blameless   1010
    and died where young men die right honorably.
    These are my instructions to communicate
    with respect to him. His brother Polynices,
    or rather his dead body, you must cast out
    unburied, for the dogs to drag and tear
    as fits one who would have destroyed our country   1015

had not some god proved obstacle to his spear.
Even in death he shall retain this guilt
against his gods ancestral whom he dishonored
when he brought a foreign host here for invasion
and would have sacked the city. So it is resolved
that he shall have, as his penalty, a burial   1020
granted dishonorably by the birds of the air
and that no raising of a mound by hand
attend him nor high-pitched singing of a dirge.
Unhonored shall his funeral be by friends.
This is the pleasure of the Cadmean state.   1025

ANTIGONE
But I to those Cadmean magistrates
declare: if no one else will dare to join me
in burying him, yet will I bury him
and take the danger on my head alone
when that is done. He is my brother. I
am not ashamed of this anarchic act   1030
of disobedience to the city. Strange,
a strange thing is the common blood we spring from—
a mother wretched, a father doomed to evil.
Willingly then with one that would not will it,
live spirit with dead man in sisterhood
I shall bear my share. His flesh
the hollow-bellied wolves shall never taste.   1035
Let that be no one's "pleasure or decree."
His tomb and burying place I will contrive
though but a woman. In the bosom folds
of my linen robe I shall carry earth to him.
And I shall cover him: let no one determine   1040
the contrary. I am resolved—I shall
find means to bring this burial to pass.

HERALD
I forbid you to act so in defiance of the city.

ANTIGONE

I forbid you your superfluous proclamations.

HERALD

Harsh are the people once the danger's past.

ANTIGONE

Go on, be harsh. But he shall not go unburied. 1045

HERALD

The city hates him: will you grace him with a tomb?

ANTIGONE

Long since the gods determined of his honor.°

HERALD

Not after he cast in peril this land of ours.

ANTIGONE

He suffered ill and was paying back what he suffered.

HERALD

This deed of his was aimed at all, not one. 1050

ANTIGONE

Of all the gods Contention has final say.
But I shall bury him: spare me long speech.

HERALD

Have your own way: but I forbid the act.

(*The First Half-Chorus stands with Antigone around Polynices' corpse.*)

FIRST HALF-CHORUS [*chanting*]
Alas, alas!
O high-vaunting ruin to the race, 1055
fatal Furies, who have destroyed
the race of Oedipus so utterly—
What will happen to me? What shall I do?
What shall I plan?
How shall I be so heartless

not to mourn for you,
not to give escort to your funeral?

(The Second Half-Chorus stands with Ismene around Eteocles' corpse.)

SECOND HALF-CHORUS [chanting]
But I fear the dreadful authority   1060
of the people: I turn to avoid that.
You shall have many mourners:
but that one, poor wretch, shall go unwept
save for his sister's single dirge.
Who would believe all this?   1065

FIRST HALF-CHORUS [chanting]
Let the city do or not
what it will to the mourners of Polynices.
We here will go and bury him;
we will go as his escort.
This grief is common to the people,
yet now one way and now another   1070
the city approves the path of justice.

SECOND HALF-CHORUS [chanting]
But we will go with the other, as the city
and justice jointly approve.
For next to the Blessed Ones and the strength of Zeus
it was he above all who saved the city   1075
of the Cadmeans from being engulfed
by the wave of foreign invaders,
and from complete destruction.]

(Exit all.)

THE SUPPLIANT MAIDENS

Translated by SETH BENARDETE

THE SUPPLIANT MAIDENS: INTRODUCTION

The Play: Date and Composition

The Suppliant Maidens was first performed in the late 460s BCE, probably 463, in a connected tetralogy of which the other plays were *The Egyptians*, *The Danaids*, and the satyr-drama *Amymone*. The order of the three tragedies is not certain, however, and only small fragments of the other plays survive in quotations from other authors. (The scanty—but striking—remains of the tetralogy are presented on p. 161.)

We know the date of performance from an ancient papyrus that was first published in the 1950s. It included the information that Sophocles (whose career as a tragedian began in 468) was awarded second prize, while Aeschylus won first. Before the papyrus was published, it had been widely believed that *The Suppliant Maidens* must have been a very early specimen of Aeschylus' work, and thus the earliest surviving Greek drama: the prominent role of the chorus (and, some argued, also its size, presuming it actually comprised fifty members) and also the use of only two speaking actors, for the most part only one at a time, were all viewed as evidence of the play's primitive character. But now that it is known that the play and trilogy were composed near the end of Aeschylus' career, we understand that the assignment of such a dominant role to the chorus (actually comprised of just twelve members, as was customary at that time) was a dramatic choice—one that Aeschylus made again in his *Eumenides*—not a matter of necessity or primitiveness; and critics have come to recognize the complex and sophisticated exploration in the play and in the trilogy as a whole of patterns and themes that often resemble quite strikingly those of the *Oresteia*, which was composed just a few years later (458).

The Myth

The saga of the fifty daughters of Danaus (the Danaids) and the fifty sons of Egyptus was well known and often retold throughout antiquity. Danaus and Egyptus were brothers, descended from Zeus and Io, the daughter of Inachus, king of Argos. Because of Hera's anger at Zeus' infidelity, Io had been transformed into a cow and forced to roam all over the world, tormented by a gadfly, until she reached Egypt, where at Zeus' touch she conceived and bore Epaphus ("Caress"), who was the grandfather of the brothers. (This story is told in *Prometheus Bound*, where Io herself appears as a character.) A quarrel arises between Egyptus and Danaus, involving (among other things) a demand by Egyptus and his fifty sons that they be allowed to marry Danaus' daughters, their first cousins. (Marriage between first cousins was accepted in most parts of the Greek world, but not in all.) Danaus flees the country with his daughters, and they seek refuge in Argos, their ancestress' home city. This is the point at which our play begins.

As suppliants in Argos, the daughters invoke the protection of the king (traditionally named Pelasgus) and of the citizens as a whole, in the name of Zeus in his capacity as Hikesios (god of suppliants), who also is one of the Danaids' progenitors. Pelasgus deliberates anxiously, worried about drawing his city into a war against the Egyptians over such an issue. But after consulting his citizens, he agrees to protect the Danaids and let them make a new home in his city. Then an Egyptian herald arrives, accompanied by soldiers, and attempts to seize the Danaids and take them forcibly back to Egypt to marry their cousins. Pelasgus returns to the scene just in time to stop this, and the play ends with the Danaids celebrating their acceptance into a new home, even as Argos prepares for war.

As for the rest of the trilogy, many details are uncertain, but we know that a battle is fought in which the sons of Egyptus are victorious, and the fifty Danaids are forced to marry them. (It is possible, but not certain, that Danaus has by now become king of Argos, Pelasgus having been killed in the battle against the Egyptians.) On their wedding night, following their father's instructions, forty-nine of the daughters stab their new husbands to death. Only one, Hypermestra, who has fallen in love with her husband, Lynceus, spares him. Danaus is angry with her for being disobedient; and conversely Lynceus seeks revenge on Danaus for the murders of his brothers. In *The Danaids*, the third play of the trilogy, the goddess Aphrodite appears and pronounces her approval of Hypermestra's loyalty to her husband and of marriage in general. Part of her speech describing the universal power of love is preserved (see p. 161), but it is unclear how the trilogy ended. Danaus may or may not have been put to death. In some versions of the myth, the Danaids remarry and live happily ever after; in others, they are punished instead, either on earth or eternally in the underworld, or both. In all versions Lynceus and Hypermestra become the ancestors of a great line of Argive kings and heroes, including Perseus and Heracles (as is again mentioned in *Prometheus Bound*).

It is uncertain whether *The Egyptians* preceded *The Suppliant Maidens* in the trilogy (in which case presumably the play's action took place in Egypt and involved the quarrel between the two brothers), or whether *The Suppliant Maidens* came first and *The Egyptians* second (in which case it probably would have included an account of the defeat of the Argive army and the subjugation of the Danaids). We do know that in the opening scene of the third play (*The Danaids*) day has just dawned and a "waking-up song" is about to greet the bridal couples (p. 161)—so presumably the murders are discovered almost immediately. What else was in the play, apart from Aphrodite's speech, is not known. As for the satyr-play, *Amymone*, that concluded the tetralogy, it is named after another daughter of Danaus, sent by her father into the countryside outside Argos to fetch water and assailed there by a satyr who attempts to rape her. The god Poseidon rescues her— and then has intercourse with her himself. She ends up being honored by a fountain created at nearby Lerna. The play thus mirrors several themes from the more serious and deadly tragedies that precede it: violent sexual pursuit, divine rescue, marriage, and the founding of several local Argive traditions.

Aeschylus' handling of the myth in *The Suppliant Maidens* raises questions that are impossible for us to answer, especially given that we lack two-thirds of the trilogy. Above all, precisely why do Danaus and his daughters so strongly resist the idea of marrying Egyptus' sons? Do they disapprove of cousin-marriage? Or do they dislike these particular men, or even men altogether? Or (as some scholars have suggested) has Danaus received a prophecy that a grandson of his will one day kill him? By itself our play presents a unique portrait of young women victimized and in fear of sexual abuse, together with intimations of potential retaliation and unexpected violence, while also demonstrating the power of formal supplication as a social and religious mechanism. Also prominent is the theme of immigration and asylum, complicated by issues of ethnic difference: whereas the Egyptian men are portrayed as crude and ferocious barbarians in contrast to Pelasgus and his calm, quasi-democratic mode of deliberation and policy making, the Danaids themselves (and the oft-mentioned figure of Io as well) are presented as a confusing mixture of exotic and Greek, pathological and normal. Are they to be seen as timid victims or deadly murderers? As helpless female objects of male domination or man-hating fanatics? Such moral ambiguities and shifts in audience sympathy are characteristic of Aeschylus' trilogic technique, as we see from his *Oresteia* and Theban trilogy as well.

Transmission and Reception

There is little evidence that *The Suppliant Maidens* or any of the other plays in its tetralogy were performed or widely read in antiquity, though several Athenian vase paintings from ca. 400 BCE depict scenes of Amymone, Poseidon, and the satyrs, perhaps based on Aeschylus' *Amymone*. It is hard to understand why

The Suppliant Maidens was selected to be among the seven of Aeschylus' tragedies that were apparently collected (we do not know by whom) as an edition for school use at some point in the Roman period, especially because a high proportion of the play is choral lyric and contains much unusual and difficult language. Perhaps it was the ethical message of the play that appealed to schoolteachers, since Pelasgus provides a model of a good Greek ruler, and the story demonstrates the importance of performing and accepting supplication. Only one medieval manuscript preserves this play, and unfortunately its text is in woeful condition: there are many places where the words have been corrupted into nonsense or into strange expressions that even the ever-experimental Aeschylus can scarcely have composed. So we are sometimes reduced to speculative emendation or mere guessing as to what was originally written, especially in some of the choral songs. Nonetheless, the dramatic power and emotionality of the play, along with its strong religious feeling, are unmistakable.

During the Renaissance and Enlightenment, the play was rarely studied or read as a viable drama. Nor does it seem ever to have been staged in theaters. German Romanticism brought increased attention, but the play was generally viewed as a fascinating but primitive museum piece, a ritual drama or lyric oratorio, interesting only for what it might reveal about the earliest stages in the evolution of tragedy: highly musical, full of moving bodies swirling around the orchestra (employing two or even three separate choruses, it appears), but lacking action and psychologically interesting characters (compared with other surviving Greek tragedies), and obsessed with Zeus and divinity. Only since the mid-twentieth century has the play come back into its own as an effective piece of theater and a drama packed with interesting ideas. Nowadays it is admired for its fierce sexual politics, arresting ethnic and racial contrasts, and brilliant stage effects—for example, the spectacle of the twelve chorus members threatening to hang themselves by their belts from the statues of the gods to cast a pollution on the city from which they are demanding asylum, while the king agonizes over what he should do.

From the early twentieth century, the most famous production of the play was the 1930 festival performance at Delphi (in Modern Greek), directed by Eva Palmer-Sikelianos, with a chorus of fifty, plus twenty-five attendants. Notable too was the version directed by Jean-Louis Barrault, with music by Arthur Honegger (Paris 1941, 1943). Since the 1960s, productions and adaptations of Aeschylus' play have been more frequent, including several by the National Theater of Greece (1964, 1968, 1977) and one by Karolos Koun and the Theatro Technis (1984). In English, the bold adaptation by Charles Mee, *Big Love; or, The Wedding of the Millennium* (1999) has been strikingly staged in productions by Les Waters (San Diego, Louisville, and elsewhere).

THE SUPPLIANT MAIDENS

Characters   CHORUS of Danaids, daughters of Danaus
DANAUS, their father; brother of Egyptus
PELASGUS, king of Argos
CHORUS of Egyptian sailors
EGYPTIAN HERALD, representing the sons
of Egyptus
CHORUS of Argive citizens

Scene: A sacred grove near Argos, adorned with an altar and statues of Greek gods.

(Enter Chorus from the side, followed by Danaus.)

CHORUS [*chanting*]
Zeus Protector, protect us with care.
From the fine sand of the Nile delta
our ship set sail. And we took flight:
from a holy precinct bordering Syria   5
we fled into exile, condemned
not for murder by a city's decree,
but by self-imposed banishment, abhorring
impious marriage with Egyptus' sons.   10
Danaus, our father, adviser and lord,
moving the counters of hope,
picked the best strategy for grief,
quickly to fly through the sea
and find anchor at Argos,   15

whence we claim we're descended
by the breathing caress of Zeus
on a cow driven wild.

    To what kinder land could we turn than this,
with our suppliant olive branches,
hand-held implements wreathed in wool?   20
This city, this earth and bright water,
and you Olympian gods, and also
those venerable gods dwelling below,   25
and Zeus Savior, the third, protector
of pious men, may you all receive
this suppliant band of maidens well,
with this land breathing solemn respect.

    But that thick swarm of insolent men,   30
before they can land on this marshy shore,
return them and their ship to the sea!
And by the winter sting of hurricane,   35
facing the wild sea, by thunder and lightning,
by rain-winds assailed may they die,
before they seize what law forbids,
as cousins to mount on unwilling beds.   40

[singing]

STROPHE A

Now I invoke
the calf of Zeus, avenger
beyond the sea:
child from the grazing
cow, our fore-mother.
Conceived by the breath and touch
of Zeus, when due time came   45
his proper name was given:
Epaphus, Caress.

ANTISTROPHE A

Him I invoke:
in pastures where our mother

suffered before;   50
I'll show a witness
faithful but unex-
pected to natives here.
They shall know the truth   55
at last and at length.

STROPHE B

And if some neighbor here knows bird cries,
hearing our bitter lament he will think
he hears the hawk-chased, sad bird Metis,   60
the wife of Tereus ...

ANTISTROPHE B

    ... who laments with passion,
barred from rivers and the countryside;
who sings her son's death dirge, whom she killed.   65
Perverse her wrath.

STROPHE C

Thus melancholy I
with Ionian songs
rip at my Nile-soft cheek,°   70
my heart unused to tears.
We gather blooms of sorrow,
anxious that a friend,
someone, will protect us,   75
exiles from a misty land.

ANTISTROPHE C

But gods ancestral, hear,
and look kindly on justice!
Don't grant youth what's not theirs;   80
show your true loathing of rape.
So you would be most righteous.°
Even from war there are havens—
an altar, defense for the weary
in exile, a respect of gods.   85

May his will, if it's Zeus', be well.
His desire is not easily traced:
everywhere it gleams, even in darkness,
with black fortune to mortals.°

ANTISTROPHE D

And so safe it falls, without slips,   90
an act fulfilled by his nod.
Dark are the devices of Zeus' counsel,
stretching out, blind to our sight.

STROPHE E

From towered hopes   95
he casts men to destruction.
He needs no armed violence;
all god's work
is effortless: seated,
calm and motionless,
from his holy throne
his will is accomplished.   100

ANTISTROPHE E

On mortal outrage
look down, how it grows,   105
the young rootstock, and swells,
eager for marriage
with us, hard to dissuade—
intent in its frenzy,
with spur inescapable,
deceived to destruction.°   110

STROPHE F

I sing suffering, shrieking;
shrill and sad I am weeping.
Ah, my life is dirges
and rich in lamentations,   115
I weep for my honor.

I invoke your Apian land.
You know my foreign tongue.
Often I tear my Sidonian veil of linen.   120

We grant gods oblations
where all is splendid
and death is absent.°
O toils undecipherable!   125
Where will these billows take us?
I invoke your Apian land.
You know my foreign tongue.
Often I tear my Sidonian veil of linen.   130

Oar blade and linen-sewn ship,
deck secure from the sea,   135
with fair winds brought me here;
nor do I blame that voyage.
May the all-seeing Father
bring a gracious end in time: 140
that the seed of that most revered
mother escape, alas,
untamed and unwed, virgin to the bed of man.

The pure daughter of Zeus,
who guards sacred walls,   145
may she guard and protect me:
virgin, rescuing virgins,
may she come in all her power:
that the seed of that most revered   150
mother escape, alas,
untamed and unwed, virgin to the bed of man.

But if not,
we, a sunburnt race,   155

[125] THE SUPPLIANT MAIDENS

shall go in supplication
to the Zeus of the dead
who welcomes all strangers,
hanging ourselves in nooses,
if Olympian gods heed not.   160

    O Zeus! Poor Io, the wrath
    that came from heaven to hunt her!
    I know the jealous madness
    of mighty Zeus' wife.   165
    From a fierce wind a storm will come.

ANTISTROPHE H

Will not Zeus
then be criticized
for his unjust neglect
of the cow's son—his own—   170
turning now his face
away from my prayers?
But on high may he hear us call!   175

    O Zeus! Poor Io, the wrath
    that came from heaven to hunt her!
    I know the jealous madness
    of mighty Zeus' wife.
    From a fierce wind a storm will come.°

DANAUS

Prudence, my daughters; prudently you came
with an aged father as your trusted pilot.
And now, with foresight, I advise you take
care to seal my words within your mind.
I see dust, the silent messenger of arms,   180
but not in silence are the axles turned.
Crowds I see, armed with shield and spear,
followed by horses and curved chariots.
Perhaps the rulers of this land have come
to meet us, informed by messenger.   185
But whether kindly purposed or provoked

to savageness they speed their armament,
it is best for us to sit as suppliants
at this rock, sacred to the assembled gods.
An altar's stronger than ramparts; it's a shield 190
impenetrable. Quickly come here now,
with white-wreathed suppliant branches solemnly
held in the left hand, emblem of august Zeus.
Mournful, respectful, answer needfully
the strangers; tell distinctly of an exile 195
unstained by murder. Let nothing bold
attend your voice, and nothing vain come forth
in glance but modesty and reverence.
Not talkative nor yet a laggard be in speech: 200
the people here are quick to take offense.
Remember to yield: you're foreign refugees,
in need, and boldness never suits the weaker.

CHORUS LEADER
With prudence, father, you speak to the prudent.
I shall take care and not forget your good 205
commands; may Zeus, our ancestor, be witness.°

DANAUS
May he look then with propitious eye.

CHORUS LEADER
Now would I wish to sit there by your side.

DANAUS
Delay not; and may our plan prevail.

CHORUS LEADER   (*Addressing the statue of Zeus*
                                 accompanied by an eagle.)
O Zeus, look down and pity us, near death. 210

DANAUS
If Zeus is willing, this will all end well.
And now invoke also this bird of Zeus.

CHORUS LEADER

We call upon the sun's rays that protect.

DANAUS

Call too on Apollo, the god once exiled from heaven.

CHORUS LEADER

Yes, knowing this fate, he should feel sympathy.   215

DANAUS

Let him sympathize, and defend us eagerly.

CHORUS LEADER

Which other of these gods must I invoke?

DANAUS

I see this trident, symbol of the god . . .

CHORUS LEADER

. . . who brought us here well: may he receive us well.

DANAUS

And that one there is Hermes, in Greek style.   220

CHORUS

May he be a good herald to us, now free.

DANAUS

Worship all gods here at their common altar.
Settle on the sacred ground like doves
clustering together, fearing the winged hawks,
who hatefully pollute their kindred blood.   225
Bird consumes bird, how could that be pure?
And how could a man, taking an unwilling
bride from an unwilling father, still be pure?
Not even in Hades will he flee the guilt
of lust: there too (they say) another Zeus   230
among the dead works out their final punishment.
Fix your eye on that, and make response:
so that victory may be with you in this action.

(Enter Pelasgus from the side, with attendants.)

PELASGUS

Whence comes this crowd of barbarians?
What shall we call you? So outlandishly   235
arrayed in this exotic luxury
of robes and headbands, not in Argive fashion
nor even in Greek? I wonder too at this: 240
how, without herald, without guide or patron,
you have yet dared to come so fearlessly.
The suppliant olive branches before these gods
you've placed—as is our custom; but nothing more
than that seems Greek: in other things I could
conjecture only, unless your voice might guide.   245

CHORUS LEADER

You spoke no lie about our dress. But to whom
do I speak? an Argive citizen, or warden
with his sacred staff, or the city's head?

PELASGUS

Answer me with trust: I am Pelasgus,
ruler of this land, and son of Palaechthon   250
the earth-born. Pelasgians bear my royal name
and reap the fruits of this earth. I rule the lands
through which pure Strymon flows, to where the sun   255
sinks in the west: our borders are Paeonia,
and beyond the Pindus, near the Perrhaebians,
and the mountains of Dodona—and then the sea:
I am the ruler of all within that frame.
The land since ancient times is called Apia,   260
after a healer, the prophet Apis, son
of Apollo, who from Naupactus once came
and cleansed this land of deadly, monstrous creatures,
serpents that the earth, soaked in old   265
curses of blood, sent forth and smeared in wrath.
He worked a cure with remedies and herbs

for Argos, and as payment he found remembrance
in our prayers. Those then are my testaments,   270
and now you must tell your own ancestry.
The city, though, is no friend of long speeches.

CHORUS LEADER
    Brief and clear is my tale: by race we claim
    to be Argives, descendants of that fruitful cow.   275
    I'll tell you how close truth clings to what we say.

PELASGUS
    You speak beyond my credence, strangers, claiming
    Argive birth: more like Libyans you seem
    than like women native here; or else the Nile   280
    might foster such a breed; perhaps such features
    might Cypriot men reproduce through their wives;
    and I've heard of Indian women riding camels
    like horses, nomads, neighbors to the Ethiopians;   285
    I should even have thought you were the man-hating
    carnivorous Amazons, were you armed with bows.
    But, once instructed, I would more fully know
    how your birth and ancestry is Argive.   290

CHORUS LEADER
    They say that Io once upon a time
    was Hera's temple priestess here in Argos.

PELASGUS
    Yes, so she was; the story is well founded.

CHORUS LEADER
    And isn't it also said that Zeus was joined   295
    with a mortal . . . ?°

PELASGUS
    .   .   .   .

CHORUS LEADER
    and this did not remain concealed from Hera.

PELASGUS

How did these royal jealousies end up?

CHORUS LEADER

The goddess changed the woman to a cow.

PELASGUS

And Zeus, did he approach the fine-horned cow?   300

CHORUS LEADER

He became a bull, they say.

PELASGUS

What did Hera do?

CHORUS LEADER

She set over the cow a guard, all-seeing.

PELASGUS

Who was this all-seeing herdsman that you speak of?

CHORUS LEADER

Argus, a son of Earth, whom Hermes slew.   305

PELASGUS

But what did Hera appoint for ill-omened Io?

CHORUS LEADER

A gnatlike goad it was, or driving sting.

PELASGUS

All that you say matches what I know.   310

CHORUS LEADER

It was what the Nile-dwellers call the gadfly.

PELASGUS

That's how the goddess drove her away from Argos?

CHORUS LEADER

Yes, and so to Canobus and to Memphis
she came, where Zeus by touch begot a son.

PELASGUS

So what is the name of this calf of Zeus?

CHORUS LEADER

Epaphus,   315
truly named Caress, from his conception.

PELASGUS

And who from him?

CHORUS LEADER

Libya, who reaped the greatest share
of Africa.

PELASGUS

And then who was her offspring?

CHORUS LEADER

Belus, who had two sons, and was the father
of my father.

PELASGUS

So tell me, what is his name,
in all its significance?

CHORUS LEADER

Danaus. And his brother   320
fathered fifty sons.

PELASGUS

Please do not grudge
to disclose his name as well.

CHORUS LEADER

It is Egypt.
So now that you know my ancient lineage,
you should offer protection to this Argive company.

PELASGUS

You seem from long ago to have a share   325
in this, our land: but what impelled you, how

did you bring yourself to leave your father's house?
What fortune swooped upon you?

CHORUS LEADER
                    Lord Pelasgus,
shifting are the ills that humans suffer;
nowhere is trouble seen of the same feather.
Who'd ever have thought that we would land in Argos,
unexpected refugees yet former natives,   330
cowering in fear of a hated marriage bed?°

PELASGUS
  Why have you come to these assembled gods,
  holding white-wreathed branches, newly cut?

CHORUS LEADER
  So as not to be a slave to Egyptus' sons.   335

PELASGUS
  Is this from hatred, or does the law forbid it?

CHORUS LEADER
  What woman could like a man she buys as her owner?

PELASGUS
  Thus greater grows the strength of human families.

CHORUS LEADER
  And when things go badly, separation is quite easy.

PELASGUS
  How then can I act with piety toward you?   340

CHORUS LEADER
  Don't give us back when Egyptus' sons demand it.

PELASGUS
  A hard request—to take on a new war.

CHORUS LEADER
  But justice gives protection to her allies.

PELASGUS

If from the start she shared in what you're doing.

CHORUS LEADER

Respect the ship of state thus garlanded. 345

PELASGUS

I shudder as I see these shaded altars:
the wrath of Zeus the Protector is stern indeed.

CHORUS [*singing now in this lyric interchange with Pelasgus, who
speaks in response*]

STROPHE A

Son of Palaechthon,
listen to me with a caring heart,
lord of Pelasgians.
Protector, behold a wandering exile:
the heifer, wolf-pursued, on steep rocks, 350
trusting in the herdsman's strength
calls out to him in fear.

PELASGUS

I see this crowd of gods assenting, each
shadowed by the fresh-cut olive branches. 355
Yet may these guests of the city bring no ruin,
and may no strife arise within the city
in unexpected and unplanned-for ways.

CHORUS

ANTISTROPHE A

Yes, may the goddess Right,
protectress with Zeus of suppliants,
see that this refuge 360
of ours does not bring ruin!
And you, though older from younger, learn:
it's wise to respect a suppliant:
the gods favor a man of pure heart.°

PELASGUS

But you are not suppliants at my own hearth.   365
If pollution stains the city now in common,
let the people all together work a cure.
I will myself not make you any promises
until I've shared this with all the citizens.

CHORUS

STROPHE B

You are the city, the people!   370
A ruler's not subject to judgment:
you rule the land, the hearth, the altar
with your single vote and scepter;
enthroned you command
and fill every need.
Beware pollution!   375

PELASGUS

May any pollution fall on my enemies!
I cannot aid you without causing harm;
yet it is not wise to disregard such prayers.
I am at a loss, and fearful is my heart
to act or not to act and take my chances.   380

CHORUS

ANTISTROPHE B

Regard him, above, the protector,
the guardian of mortals who suffer
and supplicate their neighbors
but get no proper justice.
The anger of Zeus the protector
of suppliants persists,   385
not diverted by pity.

PELASGUS

If Egyptus' sons have power over you
by your city's laws, claiming they are nearest

of kin, who would wish in that to oppose them?
You must plead your case according to your laws 390
at home, that they lack authority over you.

CHORUS

STROPHE C

Yet subject to men may I never be!
I'd follow a course right up to the stars
to make my escape from a heartless marriage. 395
Choose justice as your ally,
let your judgment honor the gods.

PELASGUS

The choice is not easy: choose me not as judge.
I said before that never would I act
alone, apart from the people, though I am ruler;
so never may people say, if evil comes, 400
"By honoring immigrants you destroyed the city."

CHORUS

ANTISTROPHE C

Both sides he surveys: of related blood
to each, Zeus is, impartial his scales.
To the evil and lawful he weighs out
the holy and unjust fairly. 405
So why fear to do what is right?

PELASGUS

There's need now of deep thinking that can save us,
plunging like a diver to the bottom,
keen and unblurred his eye, to make the end
without disaster for us and for the city; 410
that neither strife may bring reprisals, nor,
if we should give you up, seated thus
on seats of gods, we settle the god, destructive
Vengeance, in this land, who even in Hades 415
never frees the dead. Do we not seem
to stand in need of thinking that can save us?

CHORUS [*singing*]

STROPHE D

Think, and be truly
our pious protector.
Betray not the exiles,   420
pursued from afar
and cast out by the godless.

ANTISTROPHE D

See me not seized
from the many gods' seats,
O lord, this land's ruler.   425
Know the men's violence
and beware the gods' anger.

STROPHE E

Bear not to see
a suppliant by force   430
dragged from these statues,
seized by my garments
like a horse by the bridle.

ANTISTROPHE E

Do what you will,
your house and children still
remain to pay back   435
justice in full. So think:
the justice of Zeus rules.

PELASGUS

I have indeed thought, and here I'm run aground:
against you or them necessity is strained   440
for mighty war, as tightly nailed together
as a ship tied up in harbor: and nowhere
lies a painless course.

        When wealth is sacked and homes   445
are pillaged, Zeus may grant another fortune;
or when a tongue has failed to speak in season

and hearts are spurred to anger, a healing word
may spread a counterbalm: but kindred blood
is different. To avoid it, sacrifices   450
and offerings are needed, many of them
to many gods, as cures for such affliction.
So truly I am spent by this dispute:
I wish an ignorance more than the art of ills:
against my judgment may it turn out well.

CHORUS LEADER
But hear the ending of my reverent prayers.   455

PELASGUS
I heard, and please keep speaking: it won't escape me.

CHORUS LEADER
Clasps and belts and girdles we all have.

PELASGUS
Doubtless these are proper for women to wear.

CHORUS LEADER
From these, you know, there comes a fine device.

PELASGUS
Tell me, please, just what is on your mind.   460

CHORUS LEADER
Unless you promise to our company . . .

PELASGUS
What will your "device" of girdles then accomplish?

CHORUS LEADER
They'll adorn these statues with new dedications.

PELASGUS
These words seem like riddles. Please speak simply.

CHORUS LEADER
As soon as we can, from these gods we'll hang ourselves. 465

PELASGUS

I hear your words as a whip against my heart.

CHORUS LEADER

Now you grasp it: I've opened up your eyes.

PELASGUS

Ah, everywhere I'm gripped in strangleholds,
and like a swollen river evils flood.
Embarked on a sea of doom that's hard to cross   470
and bottomless, I see no saving harbor.
If I do not carry out what's due to you,
you've warned us of unmatchable pollution.
But if before these walls I take a stand
and bring the battle against Egyptus' sons,   475
your cousins, wouldn't that be bitter waste—
men to bloody the earth for women's sake?
But yet the wrath of Zeus the Suppliant—
the height of mortal fear—must be respected.

    Now then, aged father of these maidens,   480
gather those branches in your arms; and take them
to other altars of our native gods,
so none of the local people, who delight
in blame, after seeing proof of your arrival,   485
can reproach me; and perhaps they may feel pity
hating the arrogance of that masculine crowd,
and the people may feel more friendly toward you.
Everyone's kind to those weaker than themselves.

DANAUS

To have found a sponsor, reverent and kind,   490
we highly prize. And now, let local guides,
to grant me safety as I go, escort me
to the temple altars: nature made   495
my shape unlike to yours, even as the Nile
and the Inachus bear no resemblance
in their nurture. Beware lest confidence give birth
to fear: ignorance has often killed a friend.

Attend him, men: the stranger has spoken well.　　　　　　500
Guide him to the city's altars, the seats
of our gods; and say no more than this to whom
you meet: "To the gods' hearth we bring a sailor."

(Exit Danaus, attended.)

CHORUS LEADER

Him you instructed, and he is gone; but I,
how shall I act? What sign of confidence　　　　　　505
is yours to give me?

PELASGUS

　　　　　　Leave your branches here,
the symbol of your troubles.

CHORUS LEADER

　　　　　　And here I leave them
by your command.

PELASGUS

　　　　　　Toward that grove now turn.

CHORUS LEADER

But how would a public grove protect me?

PELASGUS

　　　　　　　　　　Never　　　　　　510
to rape of birds of prey shall we expose you.

CHORUS LEADER

But to those more hateful than heartless snakes?

PELASGUS

Follow my example, speak auspiciously.

CHORUS LEADER

It's not surprising for a mind to stray through fear.

PELASGUS

Excessive fear is always powerless.°

CHORUS LEADER

Soothe then my heart in word and deed, yourself.   515

PELASGUS

Your father will not long desert you; and I,
assembling all the local people, shall
make the commons well disposed, and teach
your father everything that he must say.
Now remain here, and beseech our local gods   520
with your prayers to bring about what you desire.
I shall go myself to arrange all this: and may
Persuasion and Good Fortune now attend me!

(Exit Pelasgus, with attendants.)

CHORUS [singing]

STROPHE A

King of kings, most blessed
of the blessed, most perfect strength   525
of the perfect, Zeus of all
most bountiful:
listen to us and save us,
your family, warding off
the hated violence of men.
Cast into the purpled sea
their black-benched ship of doom.   530

ANTISTROPHE A

Look on the women's side,
renew that story of kindness
from long ago, that woman,
the one you loved,
ancestress of our race.
Remember many things: 535
you touched Io.
We claim a descent from Zeus,
and from one born in this land.

To my mother's ancient track I turn:
in a rich pasture eating flowers
she was seen, whence Io   540
by gadfly driven
in frenzy escaped;
passing through many peoples,
cutting in two the land,
she defined the raging strait.   545

Rushing through lands of Asia, through
Phrygia's sheep pastures,
she passed by the city of Teuthras
and Lydian vales,   550
Cilician hills,
hurrying through fertile Pamphylia,
and its ever-flowing streams,
and the abundant land of Aphrodite.   555

She came, with the winged cowherd
still assailing her,
to the rich grove of Zeus,
a pasture fed by snow, to which
the Nile waters come   560
and Typhon's rains, by disease untouched—
herself crazed
with misery, stinging pains,
Bacchant of Hera.

And men who then lived there   565
at her strangeness trembled
with pale fear at heart.
They beheld a creature vexed, half-breed:
in part a cow

and a woman in turn, a monster marveled at.   570
Who then soothed
the wretch, wandering-far,
tormented Io?

STROPHE D

Ruling through time without end,
Zeus was the healer.°   575
By strength gentle of touch
and divine breaths
was she cured, weeping away
her grievous shame.
Bearing the burden from Zeus,   580
as it is told in truth,
she bore a blameless child.

ANTISTROPHE D

Through great time blessed
all earth shouts out,
"Of life-giving Zeus truly
this is the son." Who else   585
could cure her of that
disease plotted by Hera?
That was the working of Zeus;
and to call us "born from Epaphus"
would be truly spoken.

STROPHE E

On whom beside him   590
more justly would I call?
Himself our father, planter, worker, and lord,
craftsman of our race
long ago, all-planning.
Propitious the wind is of Zeus.

ANTISTROPHE E

Under the rule of no one   595
does he sit, inferior in power.

[143]   THE SUPPLIANT MAIDENS

He has to fear the might of nobody
enthroned above him.
His acts are quick as words.
What here does Zeus not control?

(*Enter Danaus from the side.*)

DANAUS
Take heart, my children: the news from here is good!   600
The people's vote has passed a sure decree.

CHORUS LEADER
O hail, my envoy, dearest of heralds to me!
Tell us what outcome has been authorized,
And where the populace, by show of hands,
has thrown its weight.

DANAUS
                    The Argives have decreed   605
not doubtfully, but so as to change my aging
heart to youth again; so bristled thick
the air with hands, resolving thus the law:
free we are to settle here, subject
neither to seizure nor reprisal, claimed   610
neither by citizen nor foreigner.
But if someone does use force against us, then
any citizen refusing help shall lose
his civic rights and be banished publicly.
So did the king persuade them with his speech   615
about us, citing Zeus of Suppliants—
who would fatten rich his wrath
and bring about insatiate suffering,
and how this would be for us a double defilement,   620
with regard to citizens and strangers alike.
Hearing this, the Argives, without even waiting
for the call to vote, approved it with their hands.
Pelasgus' people had heard the orator,

and easily were convinced by his directions:
but Zeus it was who authorized the outcome.

CHORUS [*chanting*]

Come then, let us offer   625
for the Argives good prayers,
a return for good things.
And may Zeus of Strangers behold
from the mouth of a stranger
offerings in true frankness,
a perfect end for all things.°

[*singing*]

And now Zeus-born gods   630
may you hear us as we pour
out prayers for our people:
that never wanton Ares
unsated of battle-cries°   635
fire this Pelasgian land,
harvesting humans
on other men's lands.

> *For compassion they showed us,*
> *and voted with kindness,*   640
> *respecting Zeus' suppliants,*
> *this wretched flock of sheep.*

Nor did they cast their votes
on the side of men,
dishonoring us women.   645
They heeded Zeus Avenger
who watches over all,
hard to fight against:
what home would desire
this avenger in its rafters?   650
Heavily he oppresses.

They respect the suppliants of Zeus,
related in blood to themselves.
So they will please the gods
with altars scoured clean. 655

STROPHE B
So out of shadowed lips let fly
honorable prayers:
never may plague
empty the city; 660
strife too never bloody
with native dead the land.°
　　Flower of youth may it ripen unplucked,
　　and partner of Aphrodite, War, 665
　　may he cut not their bloom.

ANTISTROPHE B
And laden altars, welcoming,
may they blaze up.°
Well would be ruled
cities respecting 670
above all Zeus of Strangers,
who guides by ancient law.
　　Other protectors we pray to be born 675
　　for always, and Hecate-Artemis
　　to protect birth for women.

STROPHE C
Let no murderous plague
come upon this city destroying 680
without the dance, without lyre;
arming Ares, father of tears,
and civic violence.°
　　May the bitter swarms of ill
　　far from the people sit; 685
　　and may Lycian Apollo
　　to all the youth be kind.

And may Zeus to perfection   690
bring the fruit of each season;
and many young in the fields
may pasturing cattle beget.
From the gods may they thrive in all.
   May the pious songs be sung
   at altars by minstrels;   695
   may the lyre-loving voices
   from holy lips arise.

STROPHE D

May the people, which govern the city,
protect its dignity well,
far-sighted rulers in common counsel;   700
and before going to war,
to strangers may they grant
just dealings without suffering.

ANTISTROPHE D

May the gods who possess this land
be honored always by citizens   705
with sacrifices and laurel branches.
For respect of one's parents
is third among the greatest
laws written by Justice.

DANAUS

Thank you, dear children, for these prudent prayers;   710
but from your father tremble not to hear
some unexpected news. From this outpost,
protector of suppliants, I spy that ship.
It's easy to see; nor do I fail to mark
how its sails are trimmed and sides made fast,   715
and how her bow seeks out the way with painted
eyes; and the ship, obedient, hears all too well
her tiller's governance—no friend to us!

The men on board are clear to see, their limbs
all black, their clothes white linen. Now the other
ships and the whole allied force are visible; 720
but the lead boat is close to shore, its sail
now furling, as it's rowed with steady strokes.
      So, quietly and temperately facing
this event, you must ignore none of these gods; 725
and I shall return with advocates and defenders.
Perhaps this is an envoy or a herald
coming to reclaim you as lost property.
But nothing shall happen. Have no fear of them.
Still it's best, if we should be slow to help, 730
never to forget the strength of this refuge.
Take heart. In time the appointed day will come
when he who dishonors the gods shall pay the price.

CHORUS [*singing, while Danaus speaks in response*]

STROPHE A

Father, I fear, as swift ships come;
no length of time stands between us. 735
      Terror holds me, excessive fear,
      that my headlong flight has accomplished nothing.
      Father, I am lost in fright.

DANAUS

But final was the Argive vote, my daughters;
take heart: for they shall fight for you, I know. 740

ANTISTROPHE A

CHORUS

Accursed is the mad family of Egyptus,
in war unsated: I speak what you know.
      Black ships they have, and strongly built;
      they sailed here in angry speed
      with an army large and dark. 745

DANAUS

But here they shall find many whose limbs the sun
has made quite brown and tough in noonday heat.

CHORUS

Leave us not behind, alone, father! I pray.
Women are nothing alone; no Ares is in them.
 Deadly purposed and crafty minds   750
 with impure hearts, just as ravens,
 they heed no altar.

DANAUS

Well that would be of help to us, my daughters,
if to the gods, as to you, they are hateful.

CHORUS

ANTISTROPHE B

They fear not these tridents, no awe of gods;   755
and for that they won't keep their hands from me, father.
 Arrogant with unholy rage,
 lustful and dog-hearted, obeying
 the gods in nothing.

DANAUS

A fable tells that wolves possess more strength   760
than dogs, and papyrus cannot conquer wheat.

CHORUS LEADER

We must guard ourselves against the rage
of wanton men, monstrous and profane.

DANAUS

Dispatching a naval force is never swift,
nor is its anchoring, with ropes to be secured;   765
and even safe at anchorage the helmsman
lacks courage, especially when they've come to shores
without a harbor, and the sun's given way to night.
It breeds in prudent pilots pain as sharp   770
as birth itself; nor would a host find landing
easy, before the ships take courage in
their moorings.

But you, fearful at heart, take heed
of the gods, while I, bringing aid, shall return°
to defend you: the city cannot blame
an aged messenger, youthful in his eloquence.   775

(Exit Danaus to the side.)

CHORUS [*singing*]

O mountainous land, justly respected,
what shall befall us? Where can we flee,
to a dark hiding place somewhere in Apian lands?
Black smoke might I be
bordering clouds of Zeus;   780
invisible completely
as unseen wingless dust might I die.

Disaster may be evaded no longer;°
darkness flutters in my heart.   785
My father's report dismays me: I am spent by terror.
Willing would I be
to meet my death by hanging,
before a repulsive man   790
touches my flesh: may Hades rule me first!

Where might there be a throne in the sky,
against which wet clouds become snow?
Or smooth, steep, lonely,
overhanging, distant,   795
vulture-haunted rocks,
witnessing my death-fall,
before in violence to my split heart
I meet with marriage?

I shall not refuse then to be prey,   800

a feast for dogs and native birds.
For the dead gain freedom
from lamentable ills.
Let that fate before 805
my marriage bed come!
But what means of escape can I find
to free us from marriage?

STROPHE C

Shriek and shout a cry to heaven,
proper prayers to the gods:
but how can they bring fulfilment?° 810
And father, seeing the battle,
behold with unfriendly eyes Violence,
and respect your suppliants justly,
Protector, omnipotent Zeus! 815

ANTISTROPHE C

The sons of Egyptus are proud and heartless,
men pursuing an exile,
intent on capturing me,
with shouts many and wanton. 820
But you completely,
Zeus, hold the beam of
the balance. What without you
is brought to completion for mortals?

(Enter Chorus of Egyptian sailors from the side.)°

CHORUS OF EGYPTIANS [singing in this lyric interchange, while
the Chorus of Danaids sings in response]
Oh, oh! Ah, ah! 825
We are here, to take you on our ship!

CHORUS OF DANAIDS
Before that, ravisher, would you die!
I see this beginning of my woes. 830

Ah! Escape!
They are stern-hearted in insolence,
hard to bear on land, at sea.
Lord of the land, protect us!

CHORUS OF EGYPTIANS°

Hurry! 835
Hasten to the boats
fast as you are able,
lest torn and pricked,
pricked and scratched you'll be,
bloody and bloodstained, 840
your heads cut off!
Hurry, hasten, curses! Curses! To the boats!

CHORUS OF DANAIDS

STROPHE A

If only on the flowing salt-path
you with your masters' insolence
and your bolted ship 845
all had perished!

CHORUS OF EGYPTIANS

Cease your cries! Leave your seats!° 850
Go to the ships! You without honor,
you without city, I cannot respect.

CHORUS OF DANAIDS

ANTISTROPHE A

May you never again see
that river's fruitful water, 855
whence grows the living root
and lifeblood for mortals!

CHORUS OF EGYPTIANS

I'm a soldier, of ancient family!°
Down to the ship, up on the ladder! 860
Willing, unwilling, you shall go.

CHORUS OF DANAIDS

STROPHE B

Oh, oh!
May you die helpless
across the expanse of the sea
next to Sarpedon's tomb,
piled up with sand 870
among wet breezes.

(Enter Herald from the side.)°

HERALD [*speaking to the Chorus of Danaids, who sing in response*]
Shriek and shout and call upon the gods:
but you'll not be able to escape the Egyptian ship,
however bitter your wails and shouts and groans.° 875

CHORUS OF DANAIDS

ANTISTROPHE B

Oh, oh!°
May you howl this outrage under the earth!
With your boasts overflow;
whom the great Nile might check
raging in your pride 880
and drown your violence.

HERALD

Board the swift boat at once, I order you!
Let no one delay: when we drag you by the hair
we'll have no compunction for those precious curls.

CHORUS OF DANAIDS

STROPHE C

Ah, father, to the sea he leads me; 885
like a spider, step by step,
a dream, a black dream.
O woe, woe!
Earth, mother Earth, 890
avert this fearful creature!
O father Zeus, son of Earth!

HERALD

I do not fear the gods that I see here:
they did not nurse me nor raise me to old age.

CHORUS OF DANAIDS

ANTISTROPHE C

A two-footed serpent quivers near,° 895
like a viper, bites my foot,
a poisonous thing.
O woe, woe!
Earth, mother Earth,
avert this fearful creature! 900
O father Zeus, son of Earth!

HERALD

Unless someone agrees and goes on board, that finery
you're wearing will be ripped without mercy.

CHORUS OF DANAIDS

Help—leaders of the city! I am being overpowered!° 905

HERALD

As you're not listening keenly to my words,
it seems I'll have to drag you by the hair.

CHORUS OF DANAIDS

We are done for—my lord, we suffer unspeakable wrong!

HERALD

Many lords you soon shall see—Egyptus' sons!
Take heart! You won't be complaining of lack of rulers! 910

(Enter King Pelasgus, with attendants, from the side.)

PELASGUS

You there! What are you doing? By what arrogance
dare you insult this land of Pelasgian men?
Do you think you have come to a woman's land? You are
barbarians, and you trifle insolently
with Greeks. You've made a mistake, quite lost your mind! 915

HERALD

What's my mistake? I have the right to do what I'm doing.

PELASGUS

Well, first, you don't know how a visitor should behave.

HERALD

How so? I'm just recovering what I lost.

PELASGUS

To what local sponsor did you speak?

HERALD

To Hermes the Searcher, greatest of all sponsors.   920

PELASGUS

You speak of gods but have no reverence.

HERALD

The divinities by the Nile I do revere.

PELASGUS

And these gods here are nothing, to hear you speak!

HERALD

I'll take these women, unless someone else stakes a claim.

PELASGUS

You shall regret it, and soon, if you touch them.   925

HERALD

I hear what you say—not friendly to a "visitor."

PELASGUS

I don't make friends with those who rob the gods.

HERALD

I shall go back and tell Egyptus' sons.

PELASGUS

As I guard my flock, this brings me no concern.

HERALD

But if I knew, more clearly could I tell—   930

a herald should report exactly each
particular. What shall I say? Who's he
that robs me of these cousins? Yet Ares gives
his verdict without witnesses, and doesn't settle
a suit with payment of silver: no, before that   935
many fall to the ground and kick their heels in death.

PELASGUS

Why need I tell you my name? In time to come
you and your shipmates will learn it well enough.
These women, if they were willing, you'd be welcome
to take them with you, provided that pious speech   940
persuaded them: but not against their will.°
Unanimous the vote decreed, that never
should we surrender this band of women to force.
This decision is nailed and bolted, fixed and sure: 945
not scratched on tablets, nor sealed on papyrus rolls,
you hear it announced by the tongue of freedom's voice.
Now get out of my sight immediately!

HERALD

You think it's pleasant to incite new wars.   950
May victory and rule fall to the men!

PELASGUS

And men is what indeed you will find here,
men who don't guzzle a brew of barley beer!

(Exit Herald with the other Egyptians to the side.)

Now all of you, attended by your maids,°
take heart and go to the well-protected city,   955
enclosed by towers in dense array. And many
homes there are of public property,
while I am also housed with a lavish hand:
so you may live in well-made residences
with many others; or if it pleases more,   960
you may live in a house separate from the rest.

Of these, please choose the best and most agreeable.
I am myself your sponsor, with all the citizens
whose voted will is now being fulfilled.   965
What need to wait for a greater authority?

CHORUS [*chanting*]
In return for good things,
may good things abound,
best of Pelasgians!
Kindly escort my father to here,
Danaus, prudent, brave, and wise.   970
His is the counsel where to dwell;
kindly disposed the place with good
fame and repute among the people.
Everyone's quick to blame the foreigner.
May it be for the best!

                              (*Exit Pelasgus to the side.*)

Arrange yourselves, dear maids, just as   975
Danaus instructed each of you,
as servants and part of our dowry.°

                    (*Enter Danaus from the side, with a group of*
                    Argive citizens, who form another Chorus.)

DANAUS
My children, to the Argives it is right   980
for us to pour libations, pray, and sacrifice
as to Olympian gods, since they've preserved us
wholeheartedly. They heard what had been done
and took our side, for you as relatives
reacting kindly, but bitterly against your cousins.   985
They assigned to me these armed attendants, as
a mark of honor, and so that I may not
be murdered secretly by some assassin,
an ever-living burden on the land. . . .°
       You must be grateful even more than I

for what we have obtained. So now along   990
with my other counsels inscribe this piece of wisdom:
time becomes the touchstone of the stranger,
an immigrant group in a foreign land, which bears
the brunt of every evil tongue, and is
the easy target of calumny. I beg   995
you not to bring me shame, you who have
that bloom which draws men's eyes: there is no simple
guard for fruit most delicate, that men
and beasts, both winged and footed, devour.   1000
So Cypris heralds harvests lush with love;
and every man, at the sleek allure of maidens,
as he walks by, overcome by desire,
will shoot enchanting arrows from his eyes.
After so much toil, so many seas we've ploughed,   1005
bring no shame on us now nor pleasure for our enemies.
We have the choice—a happy one—of living
either with Pelasgus, or at the city's cost.   1010
Only regard this command of your father:
value modesty more than life itself.

CHORUS LEADER

In all else may the Olympian gods bless us;
but, as for our summer's ripeness, be not anxious,
father: unless those gods have decided something new,   1015
we'll hold to the course our past intent has set.

CHORUS OF DANAIDS [*singing*]

STROPHE A

Come now to the city,
praising blessed lord gods
who shelter the city and dwell
about the ancient stream of Erasinus.   1020
Companions, take up and accompany
the song, and let praise ring
for this city. No longer the Nile
we'll respect with our hymns,   1025

but the rivers that quietly
through this land pour fullness
and gladden this earth with waters
brilliant and rich, nurturing children. 1030
May sacred Artemis see
and pity us: may there not come
compulsion of Aphrodite's goal—
a prize fit for hell.

CHORUS OF ARGIVE CITIZENS° [*singing*]

STROPHE B

But do not scorn Cypris—that is a wise rule.
Her power is nearest to Zeus, along with Hera; 1035
honored is the goddess of many wiles
in rites sacred and solemn.
Sharing with their fond mother
are Desire and Persuasion the charmer,
to whom no denial is possible. 1040
Harmony too has been granted
to Aphrodite as her province,
and whispering paths of Eros.

ANTISTROPHE B

For those who flee, harsh punishment I fear,
evil griefs and battles bloody and fierce.
Why, why did they sail so easily 1045
in swift-winged pursuit?
Whatever is destined will happen.
Infinite is the mind of Zeus,
who cannot be bypassed. 1050
To many a woman before,
marriage has come as the ending.

CHORUS OF DANAIDS

STROPHE C

May great Zeus ward off
an Egyptian marriage for me.

CHORUS OF ARGIVE CITIZENS
  That would be best, but . . .

CHORUS OF DANAIDS
  Would you charm the intractable?   1055

CHORUS OF ARGIVE CITIZENS
  The future you know not.

CHORUS OF DANAIDS
                    ANTISTROPHE C
  But how am I to plumb
  Zeus' profound mind?

CHORUS OF ARGIVE CITIZENS
  Make a moderate prayer . . .   1060

CHORUS OF DANAIDS
  What limit do you teach me now?

CHORUS OF ARGIVE CITIZENS
  . . . ask the gods nothing excessive.

CHORUS OF DANAIDS
                  STROPHE D
  May lord Zeus deprive us
  of an ill marriage
  and a bad husband.
  As Io was released from ill,   1065
  protected by a healing hand,
  his gentle force cured her.

                  ANTISTROPHE D
  And may he grant victory to women.
  I am content with two-thirds   1070
  of good, just one of ill;
  and justly, with my prayers,
  through the saving arts of god
  to follow justice.

                                        (Exit.)

THE SURVIVING FRAGMENTS OF THE REST OF THE SUPPLIANTS TRILOGY

As discussed in the introduction, we know the titles of the other two tragedies that accompanied *The Suppliant Maidens*, but not the exact order in which the three plays were performed.

From *The Egyptians*, we possess virtually nothing at all: just one word. From *The Danaids* (*Daughters of Danaus*), which certainly was the third play of the trilogy, two significant fragments are preserved in quotations by later authors. In the first (fragment 43), the speaker appears to be a servant who is approaching the bridal chambers:

> And then will come the sun's brilliant light.
> I myself eagerly, with boys and girls accompanying me,
> awaken the bridal couples, charming them
> with melodies . . .

The second passage (fragment 44) must come from near the end of the play. The goddess Aphrodite is speaking:

> As the sacred Sky longs to pierce the Earth
> so love takes hold of Earth to want that union.
> Rain falling from the teeming Sky
> makes Earth pregnant, and she brings forth for mortals
> pasture for flocks, the life-sustaining crops
> of Demeter, and the fruit-trees' harvest.
> In this rain-filled marriage she is fulfilled:
> And I myself help cause all this to happen.

The satyr-play that completed the tetralogy was *Amymone*. Although the outline of the plot is fairly certain (see Introduction, pp. 116–18), we possess only two isolated and uninformative lines.

PROMETHEUS BOUND

Translated by DAVID GRENE

PROMETHEUS BOUND: INTRODUCTION

The Play: Date and Composition

Almost nothing is known about the date or ancient performance history of *Prometheus Bound*. The play has survived to the modern era among the manuscripts of Aeschylus' plays, and until recently most scholars took for granted that it was indeed composed by him, as part of a connected trilogy. (The surviving fragments of this probable trilogy are printed below, pp. 217–21; and see pp. 168–70 for further discussion.) Some have argued that *Prometheus Bound* was a relatively early work, on the basis of its dramaturgy and style. But others have regarded it as among Aeschylus' latest compositions (which would place it in the 460s or early 450s BCE), and have compared it to the *Oresteia* for its bold trilogic worldview and religious scope.

In many respects the play is unlike any of the other six Aeschylean dramas that survive complete: the small amount and simple style of the choral lyrics, the use of actor's monody, and various other structural and stylistic features have led many scholars to conclude that Aeschylus was not in fact its author at all, or that he left the play incomplete and it was finished by members of his family. Whoever its author(s), the play and trilogy were presumably first performed at the Great Dionysian Festival in Athens, though a few scholars have suggested Sicily instead as a possible venue.

The Myth

In preindustrial societies all over the world, myths have recounted the acquisition by human beings of the divine spark of fire through a theft from the gods, usually performed by a bird or animal, sometimes by a man or even one of the gods themselves. For the Greeks, it was the pre-Olympian god Prometheus who was generally credited with this theft.

In several accounts (though this is not mentioned in our play), Prometheus was also the creator of human beings, molding them out of clay; and he was supposed to have been the father of Deucalion and Pyrrha, the two human beings who survived the great flood and repopulated the world. So Prometheus' role as a god uniquely connected and devoted to human beings seems to have been integral to his mythical personality. The etymology of his name contributed further to this: the Greeks interpreted the name Pro-metheus—probably correctly—as meaning "forethinker," whether in the sense of "thinking in advance" or "thinking on behalf of others." In cult, however, Prometheus seems to have been more specifically celebrated as a god of technology, especially of pottery, and especially in Athens, where an annual festival was held in his honor and he was worshipped in conjunction with Hephaestus and Athena.

Previous to the fifth century BCE, by far the most important literary accounts that survive of Prometheus and his interactions with Zeus and the Olympian gods come from Hesiod's two famous poems. In the *Theogony*, Prometheus tricks Zeus over the distribution of sacrificial meat between gods and humans. In retaliation, Zeus withholds (or "hides") fire from mortals, whereupon Prometheus steals and gives it to them. As punishment he is chained to a pillar and an eagle is sent to eat his liver, day after day, for centuries to come. The text seems to suggest that Heracles will eventually deliver him (with Zeus' permission) from his punishment. In the *Works and Days*, the emphasis is more on another consequence of Prometheus' repeated defiance of Zeus: the creation by Zeus and the other Olympian gods of Pandora, the first woman, as a bane of mankind. Hesiod does not state in either version why Prometheus tries to help humans in the first place: it just seems to be taken for granted. Both poems emphasize the deceptiveness of Prometheus and the greater wisdom and power of Zeus.

Doubtless other stories about Prometheus existed in abundance before Aeschylus: but none of them have survived in the literary record, though visual representations of several Promethean scenes are common from the archaic period onward. Aeschylus himself composed a satyr-drama, *Prometheus Fire-Kindler* (*Prometheus Pyrkaeus*), which was performed together with his tragedy *The Persians* in 472 BCE. Several papyrus fragments of this satyr-play survive, and a number of fifth-century red-figure vase paintings seem also to have been influenced by it, as they show satyrs dancing enthusiastically around the fire-wielding Prometheus.

Those, then, were the traditional mythical elements that our author was working with. In *Prometheus Bound*, the outline of the story differs little from Hesiod's, but its trajectory and significance have been much modified, almost inverted. Zeus is here described as a youthful and impetuous tyrant, and Prometheus' theft of fire seems to have been motivated, as he explains in the play, by an unwillingness to allow Zeus to exterminate the whole human race. Another significant alteration is Prometheus' parentage: whereas in Hesiod, Prometheus is son of a Titan (Iapetus) and thus Zeus' cousin, in *Prometheus Bound* he is himself of that older generation of Titans (hence Zeus' uncle), and his mother is the supremely august Earth-Themis—an unusual merging of these two closely related figures into one. Furthermore Prometheus in this play has prophetic powers (apparently an invention of Aeschylus), and these are vital to the drama and its sequel: for Prometheus alone knows of a destiny concerning the sea nymph Thetis, that if she has a son he will be mightier than his father. This secret becomes a crucial bargaining chip for Prometheus in his prolonged confrontation with Zeus, who lacks this prophetic knowledge. (The audience of the play is aware that the eventual outcome of the story will in fact be that the gods arrange for Thetis to marry the human Peleus instead—and their son will be the mighty Achilles. Presumably this outcome was revealed in the course of the rest of the trilogy, now lost.)

Apart from these stories about Prometheus that Athenian theatergoers would know in advance, and the particular associations that the god of pottery, technology, and crafts might have for them, they would also be familiar with the many stories of Heracles' labors and his killing of the eagle that was tormenting Prometheus. So the audience would not be surprised to find Heracles playing a major role later in the trilogy. But the author of *Prometheus Bound* has added to the mix of his play (and trilogy) a further mythological ingredient that was surely unexpected: the story of Io, the young maiden from Argos whom Zeus persistently harassed and eventually impregnated. In our play, the arrival of this tormented young woman, now half transformed into a cow and pursued by a buzzing, biting gadfly, comes as a complete surprise to both Prometheus and the audience. Io's lengthy explanation of her recent sufferings, and Prometheus' predictions to her of her future travels and eventual conception, introduce an intensely human and musical-choreographic element into a play that is otherwise dominated by divine characters and lengthy narratives; and Io's miseries, caused by the crude appetite of the new, young ruler of the gods, make an effective complement to the sufferings of the older and defiant Titan.

We do not know how the original audience responded to this play, whether they were inspired or appalled by Prometheus' defiance and the shrill accusations he levels against Zeus and his regime. His final words of indignation as the windstorm and earthquake begin to engulf him at the end of the play are exciting and disturbing. How will things end? The audience's reactions must have been shaped by the way the rest of the trilogy went: and to this we must now turn.

The Prometheus Trilogy

Our surviving play, *Prometheus Bound*, was almost certainly part of a connected trilogy of tragedies, of which the next play in sequence was titled *Prometheus Unbound* (*Prometheus Lyomenos*; more literally translated, *Prometheus Being Released*). The title of the third play is less certain. Probably it was *Prometheus Firebringer* or *Firecarrier* (*Prometheus Pyrphoros*), since a play of this title is mentioned in an ancient list of Aeschylus' dramas. Although *Prometheus Unbound* does not survive as a complete text in any medieval manuscript, more than a dozen ancient quotations or citations from the play are known, some of them quite substantial (see pp. 217-21), and as a result we have a fairly good idea of the plot and characters. For *Prometheus Firecarrier*, however, the evidence is much slimmer. And we have no idea what the title or subject was of the satyr-play that completed the tetralogy.

The most likely sequence and contents for the trilogy seem to be the following:

1. *Prometheus Firecarrier*: Prometheus steals fire from the gods and gives it to humankind. He is sentenced by Zeus to an eternity of punishment.
2. *Prometheus Bound* (our surviving play).
3. *Prometheus Unbound*: Prometheus is still chained at the beginning of the play. A chorus of Titans arrives, newly released from Tartarus by Zeus. Prometheus describes to them his miseries. Then he is perhaps visited by his mother, Earth (Gê, or Gaia), who, like Ocean in *Prometheus Bound*, tries to persuade him to be reconciled with Zeus and offers to intercede on his behalf. Heracles then enters, on his way to retrieve the Apples of the Hesperides (one of his twelve labors). Prometheus tells him about his future travels and labors; Heracles shoots the eagle that has been eating Prometheus' liver. At some point Prometheus reveals the name of Thetis, who is being (or is about to be) pursued sexually by Zeus and who (Prometheus explains) is destined to bear a son mightier than his father. Grateful for this information, Zeus approves Prometheus' release, either by Heracles or by one of the gods (perhaps Hephaestus, or Athena, or Hermes). The play and trilogy end with the institution in Athens and elsewhere of a celebratory festival and torch race, the Prometheia, and with

an explanation of why humans wear wreaths (as a token of Prometheus' former bondage).

Some scholars, however, have argued for a different sequence and reconstruction:

1. *Prometheus Bound* (our surviving play).
2. *Prometheus Unbound*: As above, except that the play ends with the release of Prometheus, and the final phase of celebrations is not included.
3. *Prometheus Firecarrier*: The festival and torch race of the Prometheia are introduced, and human beings celebrate the gift of political wisdom newly granted by Zeus (and Prometheus?).

The main objection to the first reconstruction is that *Prometheus Bound* includes extensive accounts of Prometheus' gifts to humankind, described as if for the first time. The main objection to the second reconstruction is that the contents of the third play seem rather thin, perhaps insufficient to sustain much dramatic tension and interest. Given the almost complete loss of that play, however, we must reconcile ourselves to never knowing exactly how the trilogy was organized.

Transmission and Reception

Apart from a couple of allusions in Old Comedy of the 420s BCE to scenes from the *Prometheus* trilogy, there is little evidence that these plays were widely read or performed in antiquity. The figure of Prometheus continued to be employed extensively, of course, in mythological and philosophical contexts throughout antiquity and the medieval period, but usually as the personification of "forethought" and "providence"; he was no longer presented as a fierce opponent of Zeus and the Olympian gods, nor in connection with Io.

In general, after the fourth century BCE, Aeschylus' plays were much less widely read or performed than those of Sophocles or (especially) Euripides. Many of them gradually ceased to be copied and thus faded into oblivion. But all three plays of the Prometheus trilogy appear to have been catalogued among the ninety-plus dramas attributed to Aeschylus in the Alexandrian library (third century BCE), and *Prometheus Unbound* in particular was well enough known that authors such as Cicero, Strabo, Plutarch, and Arrian could quote from it extensively. When a selected edition of seven Aeschylean plays was made at some point in the Roman period, perhaps for school use, *Prometheus Bound* was included, but not *Prometheus Unbound*—for reasons unknown to us.

The play thus survived into the Byzantine and Renaissance eras, and was included (along with *The Persians* and *The Seven against Thebes*) in the triad of plays that were copied extensively during the twelfth-fifteenth centuries. Several of the manuscripts of the play contain copious marginal comments (scholia), a few of which date back to the classical period and tell us something of what took place in the other plays of the trilogy. A few lines and phrases from *Prometheus Bound* also show up in the Byzantine cento *The Passion of Christ* (*Christos Paschôn*). But for the most part, during the early modern period the play seems to have been seldom read. "Promethean fire" was generally regarded as a symbol for the intellectual and progressive capacity of human beings, but not for any kind of defiance of the supreme deity.

With the eighteenth-century Enlightenment, this began to change, and *Prometheus Bound* emerged as a favorite inspiration for radical and antireligious authors and artists. Voltaire included in his opera *Pandora* (1740) scenes of rebellion by Prometheus and other gods against Jupiter; and the young Johann Wolfgang von Goethe wrote the first two acts of a drama (1772–74), opening with the words "I refuse!," which he never completed but adapted instead into a lyric poem, *Prometheus* (1775). By the end of the eighteenth century, scholars had collected and studied the fragments of the rest of the trilogy, and were speculating about the overall story line: in 1802 Johann Gottfried Herder composed an ambitious *Prometheus Unbound*, parts of which were later set to music by Franz Liszt (1850). Percy Bysshe Shelley developed further the notion of a Prometheus-inspired rebellion against established divine authority in his own *Prometheus Unbound* (1820). Later in the nineteenth century, both Friedrich Nietzsche and Karl Marx likewise deployed the image of the Aeschylean Prometheus as a symbol for their respective notions of human artistic and political potential, and since then numerous adaptations have carried the trend forward and into the twenty-first century.

During this time, the play has been frequently performed, in original or adapted form, often provoking bold approaches to the staging and to various possibilities for overt or implied political commentary. Performances of note include the spectacular 1927 production of the play in Modern Greek at Delphi, designed and directed by Angelos Sikelianos and Eva Palmer (parts of which were captured on film and can be viewed on video); the Greek National Theater production directed by Alexis Solomos (1976–77); the Theatro Technis production directed by Karolos Koun (1983–84); and Richard Schechner's adaptation *The Prometheus Project* (New York, 1985). A number of science-fiction novels and films have also been based, however loosely, on elements of the Prometheus story, beginning with Mary Wollstonecraft Shelley's *Frankenstein; or, The Modern Prometheus* (1816); and Tony Harrison's provocative film *Prometheus* (1998) adapted our play to address the uses and abuses of technology in modern Europe. Operas based partly on it include Gabriel Fauré's *Prométhée* (1900, revised 1914–17; with libretto by Jean Lorrain and Ferdinand Hérold), Carl Orff's *Prometheus* (Munich 1968), and Luigi Nono's *Prometeo* (1984, with libretto by Massimo Cacciari).

Overall, whoever wrote it, *Prometheus Bound* stands out as one of the most famous and starkly impressive monuments of Greek drama. Its images of suffering and resistance, and the ideas that it raises of cosmic turmoil and potential overthrow of the established order, continue to challenge and inspire artists and thinkers all over the world.

PROMETHEUS BOUND

Characters   MIGHT, a henchman of Zeus
VIOLENCE (nonspeaking character)
HEPHAESTUS
PROMETHEUS
CHORUS of daughters of Ocean
OCEAN
IO, daughter of Inachus, the king of Argos
HERMES

Scene: A bare and desolate crag in the Caucasus.

> *(Enter Might and Violence, followed by*
> *Hephaestus carrying blacksmith's tools.)*

MIGHT

This is the world's limit that we've come to;
the Scythian country, an unpeopled desert.
It's your job now, Hephaestus, to carry out
the commands the Father laid on you, to nail
this malefactor to the high craggy rocks   5
in fetters unbreakable of adamantine chain.
For it was your flower, the brilliance of fire
that enables all the arts, your flower he stole
and gave to humankind; this is the sin
for which he must pay the gods the penalty—
so that he may learn to accept the sovereignty   10
of Zeus and quit his human-loving ways.

Might and Violence, with you the command of Zeus
has found fulfilment; for you there is nothing
still left to tackle. But, for myself, I have not
the heart to bind a god who's my own kin
violently here on this wintry cliff.   15
Yet it's utterly required for me to have the heart
to do just that, for it is no light matter
to neglect or disrespect the Father's words.

           High-contriving Prometheus, son of Themis,
the goddess of straight counsel, this is not
of your will nor of mine; yet I shall nail you
to this crag in bonds of indissoluble bronze,   20
far from men. Here you shall neither hear
the voice nor see the form of any mortal.
You'll be grilled by the sun's bright fire and change the fair
bloom of your skin; then you'll be glad when night
comes with her mantle of stars and hides the sun's
light; but then the sun will scatter the frost   25
again at dawn. The pain of your present torture
will be there always to wear you down; for he
that can relieve it has not yet been born.
Such is the reward you reap for loving humans.
For you, a god, feared not the anger of gods,
but gave honor to mortals beyond what was just.   30
So in return, you'll guard this loveless rock—
standing, sleepless, never bending the knee:
many a groan and many a lamentation
you'll utter, but they will not help you; no,
the mind of Zeus is hard to soften with prayer,
and every ruler's harsh whose rule is new.   35

MIGHT
Come, why are you holding back? Why are you pitying—
in vain? Why is it that you do not hate a god

whom the gods hate most of all? Why don't you hate him,
since it was your honor that he betrayed to men?

HEPHAESTUS
Kinship has strange power, and our life together.

MIGHT
Yes. But to turn deaf ears to the Father's words—   40
how can that be? Do you not fear that more?

HEPHAESTUS
You are always pitiless, always full of ruthlessness.

MIGHT
There is no point singing dirges over him.
Don't labor uselessly at what doesn't help at all.

HEPHAESTUS
O handicraft of mine—that I deeply hate!   45

MIGHT
Why do you hate it? To speak simply, your craft
is in no way to blame for his present troubles.

HEPHAESTUS
Yet I wish this craft were allotted to someone else!

MIGHT
Everything has its burdens, except ruling
over the gods. For only Zeus is free.   50

HEPHAESTUS
I know—I can see that here! And I have no answer.

MIGHT
Hurry then. Throw the chain around him, so
the Father may not see you being slow.

HEPHAESTUS
There are the fetters, there: you can see them.

MIGHT

    Put them on his hands; now with the hammer, strike   55
    with all your strength; nail him to the rock.

HEPHAESTUS

    It is being done now. I am not idling at my work.

MIGHT

    Hammer it more; put in the wedge; leave nothing
    loose. He's clever at finding a way out
    even from hopeless difficulties.

HEPHAESTUS

    Look now, his arm is fixed immovably.   60

MIGHT

    Nail the other fast, that he may learn, for all
    his cleverness, that he's not as smart as Zeus.

HEPHAESTUS

    No one, save Prometheus, can justly blame me.

MIGHT

    Drive the obstinate jaw of the adamantine wedge
    right through his breast; drive it hard.   65

HEPHAESTUS

    Ah, Prometheus, I groan for your sufferings.

MIGHT

    Are you pitying again, and groaning for Zeus' enemies?
    Have a care, lest some day you may be pitying yourself.

HEPHAESTUS

    You see a sight that hurts the eye to see it.

MIGHT

    I see that he is getting what he deserves.   70
    Now cast the chest bands firmly around his sides.

HEPHAESTUS

    I am forced to do this; do not keep urging me.

MIGHT

Yes, I will urge you, and hound you on as well.
Get below now, and hoop his legs in strongly.

HEPHAESTUS

There now, the task is done. It's not taken long.   75

MIGHT

Hammer the piercing fetters with all your power,
for the overseer of our work is harsh.

HEPHAESTUS

Your looks and the refrain of your tongue are alike.

MIGHT

You can be softhearted. But do not blame
my stubbornness and harshness of temper.   80

HEPHAESTUS

Let us go. He has the harness on his limbs.

(*Exit Hephaestus to the side.*)

MIGHT   (*To Prometheus.*)

So now, play the insolent; now, plunder
the privileges of the gods and give them
to creatures of a day. What kind of help
can mortals offer to save you from these sufferings?
The gods misname you when they call you Forethought: 85
it's you yourself who need Forethought, by which
to extricate yourself from this contrivance.

(*Might and Violence depart to the side. Prometheus is left alone.*)

PROMETHEUS

Bright sky, springs of the rivers, swift-winged winds,
numberless laughter of the sea's waves, Earth,   90
mother of all, and all-seeing circle of the sun:
I call upon you all to see what I,
a god, suffer at the hands of gods.

[chanting]

        See with what kind of tortures
worn down I shall wrestle ten thousand
years of time—such are   95
the shameful shackles that he,
the new commander of the Blessed Ones,
has devised against me.
Ah, ah!
I groan for the present sorrow,
I groan for the sorrow to come.
When shall the time come
to ordain a limit to my sufferings?   100

[speaking]

But what am I saying? I have foreknowledge of
all that shall be; it's clearly known to me,
and none of these pains shall come as a surprise.
So must I bear, as lightly as I can,
the destiny that fate has given me;
for I know well that against necessity,
in all its strength, no one can fight and win.   105
I cannot speak about my fortune, cannot
hold my tongue either. It was mortals, humans,
to whom I gave great privileges, and
for that was yoked in this unyielding harness.
I hunted out the secret spring of fire   110
that filled the fennel stalk, which when revealed
became the teacher of each craft to men,
a great resource. This is the crime committed
for which I stand convicted, and I pay
nailed in my chains under the open sky.

[singing]

Ah! Ah!
What sound, what unseen smell approaches me,   115
god-sent, or mortal, or mingled?
Has someone come to earth's end

to look on my sufferings,
or wishing something else?

[chanting]
      You see me a wretched god in chains,
the enemy of Zeus, hated of all   120
the gods that enter Zeus's halls,
because of my excessive love for mortals.
    Ah, ah! What is that? The rustle
of birds' wings near? The air whispers   125
with the gentle strokes of wings.
Everything that comes toward me
is occasion for fear.

                     (The Chorus enters.)°

CHORUS [singing while Prometheus chants in response]
            STROPHE A
Fear not: this is a company of friends
that comes to your mountain with swift
rivalry of wings.   130
Scarcely had we persuaded our father's
mind, and the quick-bearing winds
speeded us hither. The sound
of stroke of iron rang through our cavern
in its depths, and it shook from us
shamefaced modesty; unsandaled
we have hastened on our chariot of wings.   135

PROMETHEUS
Ah, children of teeming Tethys
and of him who encircles all
the world with unsleeping stream,
father Ocean: 140
look, see with what chains
I am nailed on the craggy heights
of this ravine to keep a watch
that none would envy.

ANTISTROPHE A

I see, Prometheus, and a mist of fear and tears
assails my eyes as I see your body 145
wasting away on these cliffs
in adamantine bonds of bitter shame.
For new are the steersmen that rule Olympus,
and new are the customs by which Zeus rules,
customs that have no justice to them, 150
but what was great before he brings to nothingness.

PROMETHEUS

I wish that he had hurled me
underneath the earth and underneath
the House of Hades, host to the dead —
yes, down to limitless Tartarus,
yes, though he bound me cruelly 155
in chains unbreakable,
so neither god nor any other being
might have found joy in gloating over me.
Now as I hang, the plaything of the winds,
my enemies can laugh at what I suffer.

CHORUS

STROPHE B

Who of the gods is so hard of heart 160
that he finds joy in this?
Who is there that does not feel
sorrow answering your pain —
save only Zeus? For he malignantly,
always cherishing a mind
that does not bend, has subdued the breed
of Ouranos, nor shall he cease 165
until either he satisfies his heart
or someone take the power from him — power that's hard to take!—
by some device of subtlety.

PROMETHEUS

> Yes, there will come a day
> when he will need me, me that now
> am tortured in bonds and fetters—
> he will need me then,
> this president of the Blessed Ones—
> to show him the new plot whereby he can be   170
> despoiled of his throne and his power.
> Then not with honeyed tongues
> of persuasion will he enchant me;
> he will not cow me with his threats
> to tell him what I know,
> until he frees me from my cruel chains   175
> and pays me recompense for what I suffer.

CHORUS

ANTISTROPHE B

> You are stout of heart, unyielding
> to the bitterness of pain.
> You are free of tongue, too free.   180
> But piercing fear has disturbed my mind;
> your misfortunes frighten me.
> Where and when is it fated
> to see you reach the term, to see you reach
> the harbor free of trouble at the last?
> A disposition none can touch, a heart
> that no persuasions soften—these are his,
> the son of Cronus.   185

PROMETHEUS

> I know that he's savage, his justice
> a thing he keeps by his own standard;
> yet that will of his shall melt
> to softness in due course,
> when he is broken in the way I know;
> and though his temper now

is oak-hard, it will be softened:　　　　　　　　　　190
eagerly he'll come to meet
my eagerness, to join
in amity and union with me—
one day he will come.

CHORUS LEADER [*speaking*]
　Reveal it all to us: tell us the story
　of what the charge was on which Zeus caught you
　and punished you so cruelly with such dishonor.　　195
　Tell us, if telling will not injure you.

PROMETHEUS [*speaking*]
　To speak of this is bitterness. To keep silent
　bitter no less; and every way is misery.
　When first the gods began their angry quarrel,
　and god matched god in growing faction, some　　200
　eager to drive old Cronus from his throne
　so Zeus might rule—the fools!—others again
　eager that Zeus should never be their king,
　I then with the best counsel tried to win
　the Titans, sons of Ouranos and Earth,　　205
　but failed. They would have none of crafty schemes
　and in their savage arrogance of spirit
　thought they would lord it easily by force.
　But she that was my mother, Themis, Earth—
　she is but one although her names are many—　　210
　had prophesied to me how it would be,
　just as it was determined, and she said,
　"Not by strength nor overmastering force
　must victory be decided, but the conquest
　must be by guile." This is what I told them,
　but they wouldn't even consider it at all.　　215
　　　Then with those things before me it seemed best
　to take my mother and join Zeus's side,
　and he was just as willing as we were;
　thanks to my plans the dark receptacle

of Tartarus conceals the ancient Cronus,　　　　　　　220
him and his allies. These were the services
I rendered to this tyrant and these pains
the payment he has given me in return.
This is a sickness rooted and inherent
in the nature of a tyranny:
that the one who holds it doesn't trust his friends.　　225
　　　But you have asked on what particular
charge he now tortures me: this I will tell you.
As soon as he ascended to the throne
that was his father's, straightway he assigned
to the several gods their several privileges　　　　　230
and portioned out the power; but to the unhappy
breed of mankind he gave no heed, intending
to blot the race out and create a new one.
No one opposed these plans save I: I dared.
I rescued men from shattering destruction　　　　　235
that would have carried them to Hades' house
and therefore I am tortured on this rock,
a bitterness to suffer, and piteous
to see. I gave priority to mortals
in pity, but found none of it for myself.
Instead I'm being disciplined like this,　　　　　　240
pitilessly, a spectacle that brings
shame and dishonor to the name of Zeus.

CHORUS LEADER
　Iron-minded and made of stone would be indeed,
　Prometheus, anyone who did not sympathize
　with your sufferings. I would not have chosen
　to see them, and now I see, my heart is pained.　　245

PROMETHEUS
　Yes, to my friends I am pitiable to see.

CHORUS LEADER
　Did you perhaps go further than you have told us?

PROMETHEUS

I caused mortals to cease foreseeing death.

CHORUS LEADER

What cure did you provide against that sickness?

PROMETHEUS

I placed in them blind hopes.   250

CHORUS LEADER

                                         That was indeed
a great benefaction that you gave to mortals.

PROMETHEUS

Besides this, I also gave them fire.

CHORUS LEADER

And do creatures of a day now possess bright fire?

PROMETHEUS

Yes, and from it they shall learn many crafts.

CHORUS LEADER

Then these are the charges on which—   255

PROMETHEUS

Zeus tortures me and gives me no respite.

CHORUS LEADER

Is there no limit set to end your pain?

PROMETHEUS

None save when it will seem good to Zeus.

CHORUS LEADER

How will it ever seem good to him? What hope
is there? Do you not see how you have erred?   260
It is not pleasant for me to say you've erred,
and for you it is a pain to hear. But let us speak
no more of this; instead, look for some means
of deliverance and release from your torment.

PROMETHEUS

It is an easy thing for one whose foot
is on the outside of calamity
to give advice and to rebuke the sufferer.
I knew all this, and all that I did wrong   265
I did on purpose; I shall not deny it.
In helping mortals I brought pain on myself;
but yet I did not think that with such tortures
as these I should be withered on these cliffs,
up high, alone, on this deserted hillside.   270
      But do not sorrow for my present suffering;
alight on earth and hear what is to come
so you may know it all, right to the end.
I beg you, alight and join your sorrow with mine:
misfortune wanders everywhere, and settles   275
now upon one and now upon another.

CHORUS [*chanting*]
Willing our ears,
that hear you cry to us, Prometheus.
Now with light foot I'll leave
the rushing car and sky,
the holy path of birds,   280
and approach the rugged earth:
I long to hear the story
of your troubles to the end.

      (*The Chorus exits.° Enter Ocean, riding on a winged sea monster.*)

OCEAN [*chanting*]
I come to my destination
completing a long journey,   285
to visit you, Prometheus.
I direct my swift-winged bird
with the mind alone, no bridle.
In my heart I share the pain
for your misfortunes; you know that.

I think that it is kinship
that makes me feel them so. 290
Besides, apart from kinship,
there's no one that I hold
in higher estimation than you.
This you soon shall know for sure
and know beside that in me
there is no mere word-kindness;
tell me how I can help you, 295
and you will never say
that you have any friend
more loyal to you than Ocean.

PROMETHEUS

What do I see? Have you, too, come to stare
in wonder at this great display, my torture?
How did you have the courage to come here 300
to this land, mother of iron, leaving the stream
called after you and the rock-roofed, self-established
caverns? Was it to feast your eyes upon
the spectacle of my suffering and join
in pity for my pain? Now look and see
the sight, this friend of Zeus, that helped set up 305
his monarchy, and see what agonies
twist me, by his instructions!

OCEAN [*now speaking*]

                     Yes, I see,
Prometheus, and I want, indeed I do,
to advise you for the best, for all your cleverness.
Know yourself and reform your ways to new ways, 310
for new is he that rules among the gods.
But if you throw about such angry words,
words that are whetted swords, soon Zeus will hear you,
even though his seat aloft is far removed,
and then your present multitude of pains
will seem like child's play. My poor friend, give up

this angry mood of yours and look for ways 315
of freeing yourself from these troubles. Maybe
what I say seems to you both old and commonplace;
but this is what you pay, Prometheus, for
that tongue of yours which talked so high and haughty:
you are not yet humble; still you do not yield
to your misfortunes, and you wish, indeed, 320
to add some more to them; now, if you follow
me as your teacher, you will not rear and kick
against the rider's whip, seeing that our king,
ruling alone, is harsh and sends accounts
to no one's audit for the deeds he does.
       Now I will go and try if I can free you, 325
so you be quiet; do not talk so much.
Since your mind is so subtle, don't you know
that a thoughtless tongue is subject to correction?

PROMETHEUS

I envy you, that you stand so clear of blame, 330
yet shared and dared in everything with me!
Now let me be, and do not get involved.
Do what you will, you'll never persuade him!
He is not easily won over: look,
take care you are not harmed for your journey here.

OCEAN

By nature you're much better at advising 335
others than yourself. I take my cue
from deeds, not words. Do not restrain me now
when I am eager to go to Zeus. I'm sure,
I'm sure that he will grant this favor to me,
to free you from these torments you have now.

PROMETHEUS

I thank you and will never cease; for eagerness 340
is not what you are wanting in. Don't trouble,
for you will trouble to no purpose, and no help

to me—even if you really do want to trouble.
No, rest yourself, keep out of the way;
just because I'm unlucky I would not, 345
for that, have everyone else be unlucky too.
No, for my heart is sore already when
I think about my brothers' fortunes—Atlas,
who stands to westward of the world, supporting
the pillar of earth and heaven on his shoulders, 350
a load beyond all bearing; also Typhon,
the earthborn dweller in that Cilician cave,
whom I saw and pitied, a hundred-headed monster,
dreadful, yet conquered and brought low by force.°
Once against all the gods he stood, opposed, 355
hissing out terror from his grim jaws; his eyes
flashed gorgon-glaring lightning as he thought
to smash the sovereign tyranny of Zeus.
But down upon him came the unsleeping bolt
of Zeus, the lightning-breathing flame, onrushing,
which hurled him from his high aspiring boasts. 360
Struck to the heart, his strength was blasted dead
and burnt to ashes; now a sprawling mass
useless he lies, hard by the narrow seaway
pressed down beneath the roots of Aetna. High 365
above him on the mountain peak the smith
Hephaestus works at the anvil. Yet one day
there shall burst out rivers of fire, devouring
with savage jaws the fertile, level plains
of Sicily with their fair fruits; such wrath
boiling with weapons of fire-breathing surf, 370
an unapproachable torrent, shall Typhon vomit,
though Zeus's lightning's left him but a cinder.
            But all of this you know: you don't need me
to be your teacher; reassure yourself
as you know how—this cup I shall drain myself 375
until the high mind of Zeus shall cease from anger.

OCEAN

So do you not know, Prometheus, that words
are healers of a temper that is sick?

PROMETHEUS

Yes, if one tries at just the right moment
to soften the heart, and doesn't violently
seek to reduce the anger that's still swelling.   380

OCEAN

Tell me, what danger do you see for me
in loyalty to you, and courage therein?

PROMETHEUS

I see just useless effort—and silly good nature.

OCEAN

Allow me then to be sick of this sickness, since
it's profitable, if one's wise, to seem foolish.   385

PROMETHEUS

This shall seem to be *my* fault, more than yours.

OCEAN

Clearly your words send me home again.

PROMETHEUS

Yes, lest your grieving for me bring you enemies.

OCEAN

The one who newly sits on the all-powerful throne?

PROMETHEUS

Yes, his is a heart you should beware of vexing.   390

OCEAN

Your own misfortune's my teacher, Prometheus.

PROMETHEUS

Off with you, then! Begone—keep your present mind.

OCEAN

These words fall on very responsive ears.
Already my four-legged bird is pawing the air,
the level track of heaven, with his wings,   395
and he'll gladly bend the knee in his own stable.

(Exit Ocean. The Chorus reenters from the side.)°

CHORUS [*singing*]

STROPHE A

I cry aloud, Prometheus, and lament your bitter fate,
my tender eyes are trickling tears,
their fountains wet my cheek.   400
With these cruel things done by his own private laws,
Zeus the tyrant shows his haughtiness
of temper toward the gods that were of old.   405

ANTISTROPHE A

Now all the earth has cried aloud, lamenting:
they lament what was magnificent of old,
in sorrow for your fall and for your brethren's fall.°   410
All the mortals who in holy Asia hold
their stablished habitation, all lament
in sympathy for your most grievous woes,

STROPHE B

and the dwellers in the land of Colchis,   415
maidens, fearless in the fight,
and the host of Scythia, living
round the lake Maeotis, living
on the edges of the world,

ANTISTROPHE B

and Arabia's flower of warriors   420
and the craggy fortress keepers
near Caucasian mountains, fighters
terrible, crying for battle,
brandishing sharp-pointed spears.

Only one other of the Titans have I seen 425
before this day, in torture and in bonds
unbreakable, god though he was,
Atlas, whose strength and might
were surpassing; now he bends his back
and groans beneath the load of earth and heaven.° 430

ANTISTROPHE C

The wave cries out as it breaks into surf;
the depth cries out, lamenting you; the dark
Hades, the hollow underneath the world,
sullenly groans below; the springs
of sacred flowing rivers all lament
the pain and pity of your suffering. 435

PROMETHEUS

Don't think I'm silent out of pride or stubbornness:
in self-awareness my heart is gnawed away
to see myself insulted as I am.
Yet who was it but I who distributed 440
their honors to these new gods? I'll say no more
of this; you know it all; but hear what troubles
there were among mortals, how I found them mindless
but made them intelligent and masters of their minds.
I'll tell you this, not blaming human beings, 445
but to explain the goodwill of my gifts.
For humans in the beginning had eyes but saw
to no purpose; they had ears but did not hear.
Like the shapes of dreams they dragged through their long
    lives
and muddled everything haphazardly. 450
They did not know how to build brick houses
to face the sun; nor how to work in wood.
They lived beneath the earth like swarming ants,
in sunless caves. For them there was no secure
token for telling winter or flowering spring, 455

nor summer with its crops; and all they did
they did without intelligent calculation
until I showed them the rising of the stars,
and the settings, hard to observe. And I invented
numbers for them, preeminent among all skills.
and the combining of written letters as a means   460
of remembering all things, the Muses' mother,
skilled in craft. It was I who first yoked beasts
to be slaves in harness and under pack saddles,°
as substitutes for humans in hard tasks;
and I harnessed to the carriage obedient horses,   465
the crowning pride of wealth and luxury.
It was I and none other who discovered ships,
sail-winged wagons that bear men over the sea.
Such—to my misery—were the devices which
I discovered for mortals, but I have no clever means   470
to rid myself of my own present affliction.

CHORUS LEADER
You have suffered terribly. Bewildered in your mind
you are astray, and like a bad doctor who
has fallen sick, you have lost heart not finding
by what drugs your own illness might be cured.   475

PROMETHEUS
If you hear the rest you will marvel even more
at the crafts and the resources I contrived.
Greatest was this: when one of mankind fell sick
there was no defense for him—neither healing food
nor drink nor unguent; for lack of cures they wasted,   480
until I showed them the blending of mild remedies
with which they drive away all kinds of sickness.

The many ways of prophecy I charted;
I was the first to judge what out of dreams
came truly real; and for mankind I gave meaning   485
to ominous cries, hard of interpretation,

and to the significance of road encounters.
The flight of hook-taloned birds I analyzed,
which of them were in nature propitious
and which unlucky; what habits each species has,   490
what are their hates and loves and affiliations.
     Also I taught of the smoothness of the entrails
and what color the bile should have to please the gods,
and the dappled symmetry of the liver lobe.   495
It was I who burned the thigh bones wrapped in fat
and the long shank bone; I set mortals on the road
to the murky craft of divination, making
the flaming signs, once dim, now clear to see.
So much for these things. Then beneath the earth   500
those hidden blessings, copper, iron, silver,
and gold—who can claim to have discovered them before me?
No one, I am sure, who wants to speak to the purpose.
In one short sentence understand it all: 505
all human arts come from Prometheus.

CHORUS LEADER
  Well, don't help mortals beyond due occasion
  while careless of yourself in your own troubles.
  I am of good hope that you, freed of these bonds,
  will one day be no less in power than Zeus.   510

PROMETHEUS
  Not yet has fate that brings all things to pass
  determined this. First I must be tormented
  by ten thousand pangs and agonies, as I am now,
  before I can escape my chains.
  Craft is far weaker than necessity.

CHORUS LEADER
  Who then is the steersman of necessity?   515

PROMETHEUS
  The three-formed Fates and the remembering Furies.

CHORUS LEADER

And is Zeus, then, weaker than these?

PROMETHEUS

Yes,

for he too cannot escape what is fated.

CHORUS LEADER

But what is fated for Zeus save eternal rule?

PROMETHEUS

You cannot know that yet; do not entreat me.   520

CHORUS LEADER

This must be some solemn secret that you're hiding.

PROMETHEUS

Think of some other story; this one's not seasonable
to utter, it must be wholly hidden.
For only by so keeping it can I
escape my shameful bonds and agonies.   525

CHORUS [*singing*]

STROPHE A

May Zeus never, Zeus that controls
the whole universe, oppose
his power against my mind;
may I never be lazy
or slow to give my worship at   530
the sacrificial feasts
when the bulls are killed beside
the quenchless stream of father Ocean;
may I never sin in word;
may these precepts still abide
in my mind nor melt away.   535

ANTISTROPHE A

It is a sweet thing to draw out

a long, long life in cheerful hopes,
and feed the spirit in the bright
benignity of happiness;
but I shudder when I see you 540
wasted with ten thousand pains,°
all because you did not tremble
at the name of Zeus: your mind
was yours, not his, and at its bidding
you regarded mortal beings
too high, Prometheus.

STROPHE B

Kindness that can't be requited—tell me, where 545
is the help in that, my friend? What support
in creatures of a day? You did not see
the feebleness that draws its breath in gasps,
a dreamlike feebleness by which the race
of humans is held in bondage, a blind prisoner. 550
So the plans of mortals shall never
surpass the ordered law of Zeus.

ANTISTROPHE B

This I have learned while I looked on your fortunes,
these deadly pains of yours, Prometheus.
A dirge for you came to my lips, so different
from the other song I sang to crown your marriage, 555
in honor of the bath and of the bed,
upon the day you won her with your gifts°
to be your wife—my sister, Hesione,
and so you brought her home to share your bed. 560

(Enter Io from the side, with horns like an ox on her head.)

IO [*chanting*]
What land is this? What race of men?
Who is it I see here being tortured
in rocky bondage? What is the crime

he's paying for? Tell me, to what part
of the world have my wanderings brought me?   565

[*singing*]
O, O, O,
there it is again, there again — it stings me,
the gadfly, the ghost of earthborn Argus;
keep it away, keep it away!
I'm frightened when I see the shape of Argus,
Argus the herdsman with ten thousand eyes.
He stalks me with his crafty eyes; he died,
but the earth didn't hide him; still he comes   570
even from the depths of the underworld to hunt me:
he drives me starving by the sands of the sea.

STROPHE A

The loud reed pipes, glued with wax,
drone their sleep-giving melody: 575
O, O, O!
Where am I brought by my far-wandering wanderings?
Son of Cronus, what fault, what fault
did you find in me that you should yoke me
to a harness of misery like this, O, O,
that you should torture me so to madness   580
driven in fear of the gadfly?
Burn me with fire; hide me in earth; cast me away
to monsters of the deep for food; but do not
begrudge me the granting of this prayer, King.
Enough have my much-wandering wanderings   585
exercised me; I cannot find
a way to escape my troubles.
Do you hear the voice of the cow-horned girl?

PROMETHEUS [*speaking*]
Surely I hear the voice of the gadfly-haunted
daughter of Inachus, who fired with love   590
the heart of Zeus and now through Hera's hate
is violently driven on courses overlong.

IO [*still singing*]

ANTISTROPHE A

How is it you speak my father's name?
Tell me, who are you? Who are you? Oh
who are you that so exactly accosts me by name? 595
You have spoken of the disease that the gods have sent to me
which wastes me away, pricking with goads,
so that I am moving always
tortured and hungry, wild bounding.
Quick-sped I come, 600
a victim of Hera's jealous plots.
Who has been so wretched, O, O,
before me, as to suffer as I do?
But declare to me clearly
what I have still to suffer, what would avail 605
against my sickness, what drug would cure it.
Tell me, if you know:
tell me, declare it to this unlucky, wandering girl.

PROMETHEUS

I shall tell you clearly all that you would know,
weaving no riddles, but simply, in plain words, 610
as it is just to open one's lips to friends.
You see Prometheus, giver of fire to men.

IO [*now speaking*]

You that have shown yourself a shared blessing
to all mankind, unhappy Prometheus,
for what are you being punished in this way?

PROMETHEUS

I have just now ceased from telling my mournful tale. 615

IO

Then will you grant me this favor?

PROMETHEUS

Say what it is
you are requesting; you will learn it all.

IO

Tell who it was that nailed you to the cliff.

PROMETHEUS

The plan was Zeus', but it was Hephaestus' hand.

IO

What was the offense for which this is the punishment? 620

PROMETHEUS

It's enough that I have told you clearly so far.

IO

In addition, then, indicate to me what date
will be the limit of my wanderings.

PROMETHEUS

Better for you not to know this than to know it.

IO

Don't hide from me what I am due to suffer. 625

PROMETHEUS

It's not that I begrudge you this favor that you ask.

IO

Why then delay to tell me everything?

PROMETHEUS

No grudging, but I hesitate to break your spirit.

IO

Do not have more thought for me than I want myself.

PROMETHEUS

Since you're so eager, I must speak; hear me. 630

CHORUS LEADER

Not yet. Give to me, too, a share of pleasure.
First let us question her about her sickness,
and let her tell us of her ruinous fortunes.
Then she can learn from you her sufferings to come.

PROMETHEUS

It is your task, Io, to gratify these spirits,   635
who are moreover your father's sisters. For
wailing and lamenting one's ill fortune,
when one will win a tear from those who listen,
is well worthwhile.

IO

I know not how I should distrust you; clearly   640
you will hear all you want to know from me.
Yet I'm ashamed to speak about that storm,
god-sent, that ruin of my beauty, and
how it came upon me. There were constant
night visions that kept haunting me and coming   645
into my maiden chamber and exhorting
with winning words, "O maiden greatly blessed,
why are you still a virgin, you who might
make marriage with the greatest? Zeus is stricken
with desire for you; he's afire to try the act
of love with you; do not disdain the bed   650
of Zeus. Go, child, to Lerna's grassy meadow,
to where your father's flocks and cattle stand
so that Zeus's eye may cease from longing for you."
With such dreams I was cruelly beset   655
night after night until I took the courage
to tell my father of my nightly dreams.
He sent to Pytho many an embassy
and to Dodona seeking to discover
what deed or word of his might please the gods;   660
but those he sent came back with riddling oracles
dark and beyond the power of understanding.
At last the word came clear to Inachus
charging him plainly that he cast me out
of home and country, drive me out unsupervised   665
to wander to the limits of the world;
if he should not obey, the oracle said,

the fire-faced thunderbolt would come from Zeus
and wipe out his whole race. These were the oracles
of Loxias, and Inachus obeyed them.
He drove me out and shut his doors against me   670
with tears on both our parts, but Zeus's bridle
compelled him to do this against his will.
Immediately my form and mind were changed
and all distorted; as you see, with horns,
pricked on by the sharp-biting gadfly, leaping   675
in frenzied jumps I ran beside the river
of Cerchnea, good to drink, and Lerna's spring.
The earth-born herdsman Argus followed me
whose fierceness knew no limits, and he spied
after my tracks with all his hundred eyes.
Then an unlooked-for doom, descending suddenly,   680
took him from life; I, driven by the gadfly,
that god-sent scourge, am driven always onward
from one land to another. That is my story.
If you can tell me what remains for me,
tell me, and do not out of pity try
to soothe me with kindly lies; there is no sickness   685
more shameful in my view than made-up words.

CHORUS [*singing*]
  Hold! Keep away! Alas!
  never did I think that such strange
  words would come to my ears;
  never did I think such intolerable   690
  sufferings, an offense to the eye,
  shameful and frightening, so
  would chill my soul with a double-edged point.
  Ah, ah, what a fate!
  I shudder when I look on Io's fortune.   695

PROMETHEUS
  You groan already; you are full of fear too soon:
  wait till you hear besides what's still to come.

  Speak, tell us to the end. For the sick it is sweet to know
  beforehand clearly the pain that still remains.

PROMETHEUS
  The first request you made of me you gained   700
  lightly: from her you wished to hear the story
  of what she suffered. Now hear what still remains,
  what sufferings this girl must yet endure
  from Hera. Do you listen, child of Inachus,   705
  hear and lay up my words within your heart
  so you may know the limits of your journey.
  First turn to the sun's rising and walk on
  over the fields no plough has broken; then
  you will come to the nomad Scythians, who live
  in wicker houses built on well-wheeled wagons,
  aloft; they are armed with bows that strike from far.   710
  Do not draw near them; rather let your feet
  skirt the rocky coast where the waves moan,
  and pass through their country; on your left there live
  the Chalybes who work with iron: these   715
  you must beware of; for they are not gentle,
  not people whom a stranger dare approach.
  Then you will come to the River Insolence
  that well deserves its name, but do not cross it—
  it is not a stream that can be easily forded—
  until you come to Caucasus itself,
  the highest of mountains, where the river's strength   720
  gushes from its summit. So you must
  cross its peaks, the neighbors of the stars,
  and take the road southward until you reach
  the man-hating Amazons, who one day
  shall live around Thermodon in Themiscyra   725
  where Salmydessus stands, that rocky cape,
  hostile to sailors, stepmother of ships.
  The Amazons will set you on your way

and gladly; you will reach Cimmeria,   730
the isthmus, at the narrows of the lake.
Leave this with a bold heart and then traverse
the channel of Maeotis, and hereafter
for all time men shall talk about your crossing,
and they shall call the place for you Cow's-Ford.
Leave Europe's mainland then, and enter Asia.   735

(To the Chorus.)

Do you not think the tyrant of the gods
is equally brutal in all the things he does?
He is a god, yet sought to lie in love
with this girl who's mortal, and on her he's brought
this curse of wanderings. Bitter indeed, poor girl,
you've found this suitor for your favors. Yet   740
you still must think of all that I have told you
as only the prelude.

IO
Oh, oh!

PROMETHEUS
Again, you are crying and lamenting: what
will you do when you hear of the evils yet to come?

CHORUS LEADER
Is there more suffering to come that you must tell her?   745

PROMETHEUS
A wintry sea of agony and ruin.

IO
What good is life to me then? Why do I not throw
myself at once from this rough crag, to strike
the ground and find release from all my troubles?   750
It would be better to die once for all
than suffer all one's days.

PROMETHEUS

You'd find it hard to bear these trials of mine,
since for me death is not decreed at all.
Death would be indeed release from pain;
but for me there is no limit of suffering set   755
till Zeus shall fall from power.

IO

                         And is that possible?
You mean that Zeus' rule might one day fall?

PROMETHEUS

You would be glad, I think, to see that outcome.

IO

Of course, since it's from Zeus I suffer so.

PROMETHEUS

Then know that this is truly how things are.°   760

IO

Who will despoil him of his sovereign scepter?

PROMETHEUS

His own light-witted decisions will undo him.

IO

How? Tell me, if there is no harm to telling.

PROMETHEUS

He'll make a marriage that one day he'll regret.

IO

With god or mortal? Tell me, if it may be told.   765

PROMETHEUS

Why ask what marriage? That is not to be spoken.

IO

Is it from his wife that he shall lose his throne?

PROMETHEUS

Yes, she'll bear him a son mightier than his father.

IO

And has he no escape from this downfall?

PROMETHEUS

None, save myself—if I'm freed from my chains.   770

IO

But who is there to free you, against Zeus's will?

PROMETHEUS

It has to be one of your own descendants.

IO

What, shall a child of mine free you from torment?

PROMETHEUS

Yes, in the thirteenth generation to come.

IO

No longer can I grasp your prophecy.   775

PROMETHEUS

Then do not seek to learn your own troubles further.

IO

Don't offer me the gift and then withhold it.

PROMETHEUS

I'll give you then just one of the two stories.

IO

Which stories? Say, and let me have the choice.

PROMETHEUS

Yes, I will give that to you: either to tell you   780
clearly the rest of your troubles, or my deliverer.

CHORUS LEADER

Please, grant her the one and grant me the other favor;
don't disappoint us. Tell her what remains

of her wanderings in the future; and tell us
of your deliverer. That is what I want.   785

PROMETHEUS
Since you have so much eagerness, I will not
refuse to tell you all that you have asked me.
First to you, Io, I shall tell the tale
of your sad wanderings, rich in groans—inscribe
the story in the tablets of your mind.
     When you shall cross the channel that divides   790
Europe from Asia, turn to the rising sun,
and cross the sun-scorched plains, that waveless sea,°
until you arrive into the Gorgon land
and the flat stretches of Cisthene's country.
There live the ancient maids, children of Phorcys:
three swan-formed hags, with but one common eye,   795
single-toothed monsters, such as nowhere else
the sun's rays look on nor the moon by night.
Near are their winged sisters, the three Gorgons,
with snakes to bind their hair up, mortal-hating—
no mortal that looks on them shall still draw breath—   800
this is the garrison I tell you of.
Hear, too, of yet another gruesome sight,
the sharp-toothed hounds of Zeus, that have no bark,
the griffins—beware of them!—and the host
of one-eyed Arimaspians, horse-riding,   805
that live around the waters that flow with gold,
of the River Pluto: do not go near them.
A land far off, a nation of black people,
these you shall come to, men who live hard by
the fountain of the sun where is the river
Aethiops—travel by its banks along   810
to a cataract where from the Bybline hills
the Nile pours its holy, healthful waters.
This river shall be your guide to the three-cornered
land of Nilotis, and there, by fate's decree,

there, Io, you shall find your distant home,   815
a colony for you and your descendants.
If anything of this is still obscure
or difficult, ask me again and learn
clearly: I have more leisure than I wish.

CHORUS LEADER
If there is anything further or left over
you have to tell her of her deadly traveling,
tell it. If that is all, grant us in turn
the favor we asked for earlier. You remember?   820

PROMETHEUS
The limit of her wanderings she now
has heard, complete; but so that she may know
that she has not been listening to no purpose
I shall recount what she endured before   825
she came to us here: this I give as pledge,
a witness to the good faith of my words.
    The great part of the story I omit
and come to the last stage of your wanderings.
When you had come to the Molossian plains
around the steep ridge of Dodona, where   830
the oracular seat is of Thesprotian Zeus,
the talking oaks, a wonder past belief:
by them full clearly, in no riddling terms,
you were hailed Zeus' glorious wife-to-be.
Does any of this wake sweet memories?   835
Then, goaded by the gadfly, on you hastened
by the shoreline path to the great Gulf of Rhea.
But then in backward course, as if storm-driven,
you had to reverse your tracks; in time to come
that inlet of the sea shall bear your name
and shall be called Ionian, a memorial   840
to all men of your journeying; these are proofs
for you, of how my mind sees something farther
than what is visible.

For what is left,
to you and to her this I shall say in common,
taking up again the track of my old tale.   845
There is a city, on the furthest edge of land,
Canobus, near the mouth and issuing point
of the Nile: it's there that Zeus shall restore your mind,°
touching you with a hand that brings no fear,
and through that touch alone shall come your healing.
You shall bear Epaphus, dark of skin, his name   850
recalling Zeus's touch and his begetting.
This Epaphus shall reap the fruit of all
the land that is watered by the broad-flowing Nile.
From him five generations, and again
to Argos they shall come, against their will,
in number fifty, women, fleeing from
a marriage with their cousins; but these cousins,   855
their hearts with lust aflutter, just like hawks
barely outdistanced by fleeing doves, will come
hunting a marriage that's not theirs to hunt;
the gods shall grudge the men these women's bodies,
and the Pelasgian earth shall welcome them°   860
in death, for death shall claim them in a fight
where women strike in the dark, a murderous vigil.
Each wife shall rob her husband of his life
dipping in blood her two-edged sword; even so
may Cypris come, too, upon my enemies.
But one of these girls, softened by love's charms,   865
will spare her bedfellow, her purpose blunted;
and she shall make her choice—to bear the name
of coward and not murderer, and she
shall bear in Argos a family of kings.
To tell this clearly needs a longer story,   870
but from her seed shall spring a man renowned
for archery, and he shall set me free.

Such was the prophecy which ancient Themis
my Titan mother opened up to me;
but how and by what means it shall come true   875
would take too long to tell, and if you heard,
the knowledge would not profit you.

IO [*chanting*]
Eleleu, eleleu!
It grabs me again, the twitching spasm,
the mind-destroying madness, burning me up,
as the gadfly's sting pricks like fire;°   880
my heart in its fear knocks on my breast.
There's a dazing whirl in my eyes as I run
out of my course driven by the wild winds
of maddening frenzy; my tongue ungoverned
babbles, the words in a thick muddy flow
crash into the waves of hateful ruin   885
without aim or sense.

(Exit Io to the side.)

CHORUS [*singing*]

STROPHE A

A wise man indeed he was
that first in judgment weighed this word
and gave it tongue: the best by far
it is to marry in one's rank and station;   890
let no one working with his hands aspire
to marriage with those lifted high in pride
because of wealth or ancestral glory.

ANTISTROPHE A

Never, never may you see me,
O you Fates, drawing close°   895
to the bed of Zeus, to share it as his partner,
nor ever may I be joined with a god for my wooer.
I feel dread when I see Io, hating her husband,
her virginity ravaged, in bitter wandering
because of Hera's fierce wrath.   900

But when a match has equal partners
then I fear not; may the eye
inescapable of the mighty gods
not look on me with desire.
That is a fight that none can fight, a fruitful
source of fruitlessness. I would not
know what I could do; I cannot see   905
how I would escape the plans of Zeus.

PROMETHEUS

Yet shall this Zeus, for all his arrogance,
be humble yet: such is the match he plans,
a union that shall drive him from his power
and from his throne, out of the sight of all.   910
So shall at last the final consummation
be brought about of father Cronus' curse
which he, driven from his ancient throne, invoked
against the son deposing him; no one
of all the gods save I alone can tell
a way for him to avoid such troubles: I
do know this, and how. So let him confidently   915
sit on his throne and trust his heavenly thunder
and brandish in his hand his fiery bolt;
nothing shall all of this avail against
a humiliating and intolerable fall.
Such is the wrestler that Zeus is setting up   920
against himself, a monster hard to fight.
This enemy shall find a fire to best
the lightning bolt, a thunderclap to excel
the thunderclap of Zeus; and he shall shatter
Poseidon's trident, with quakes on sea and land.   925
So, in his crashing fall shall Zeus discover
how far apart are rule and slavery.

CHORUS LEADER

What you want for Zeus is what you're stating as fact.

PROMETHEUS

They are my wishes, yet what shall come to pass.

CHORUS LEADER

So should we expect someone to conquer Zeus? 930

PROMETHEUS

Yes; Zeus will suffer worse than I do now.

CHORUS LEADER

Have you no fear of uttering such words?

PROMETHEUS

Why should I fear, since death is not my fate?

CHORUS LEADER

But he might give you pain still worse than this.

PROMETHEUS

Then let him do so; all this I expect. 935

CHORUS LEADER

Wise are the worshippers of Necessity.

PROMETHEUS

Worship, pray; flatter whatever king
is king today; but I care less than nothing
for Zeus. Let him do just as he likes; 940
let him be king for his short time: he won't
be king of the gods for long.

But look, here comes
the footman of Zeus, that fetch-and-carry messenger
of the new king. Certainly he has come here
with news for us.

(Enter Hermes from the side.)

HERMES

You, subtle spirit, you
bitter and overbitter, you that sinned 945
against the immortals, giving honor to

the creatures of a day, you thief of fire:
the Father has commanded you to say
what marriage of his is this you brag about
that shall drive him from power—and declare it
in detail and no riddles. You, Prometheus,
don't cause me a double journey; you can see   950
that Zeus is not softhearted in such matters.

PROMETHEUS

Your speech is pompous sounding, full of pride,
as fits the lackey of the gods. You are young
and young your rule, and you think the citadel   955
in which you live is free from sorrow. From it
have I not seen two previous tyrants fall?
The third, who now is king, I shall see too
fall, of the three most suddenly, most dishonored.
Do you think that I will cower before these gods,   960
—so new—and tremble? I am far from that.
Hurry away, back on the road you came.
You shall learn nothing that you ask of me.

HERMES

By previous obstinacy just like this
you've brought yourself to these your present torments.   965

PROMETHEUS

Be sure of this: when I measure my misfortune
against your slavery, I would not change.

HERMES

It is better, I suppose, to be a slave
to this rock, than Zeus's trusted messenger!

PROMETHEUS

.   .   .   .
Thus should one insult the insolent!°   970

HERMES

You seem to revel in your present state.

PROMETHEUS

Revel? I wish my enemies reveled so—
and you are one that I surely count among them.

HERMES

Oh, you would blame me too for your calamity?

PROMETHEUS

In a single word, I hate all of the gods   975
that unjustly returned me ill for good.

HERMES

Your words declare you mad, and mad indeed.

PROMETHEUS

Yes, if it's madness to detest my enemies.

HERMES

No one could bear you if you were successful.

PROMETHEUS

Alas!

HERMES

                    Alas? Zeus does not know that phrase.   980

PROMETHEUS

But time in its aging course teaches all things.

HERMES

Yet you have not yet learned a wise discretion.

PROMETHEUS

True: or I wouldn't be speaking to a servant.

HERMES

It seems you will not grant the Father's wish.

PROMETHEUS

I should be glad, indeed, to requite his kindness!   985

HERMES

You mock me like a child!

PROMETHEUS

              And are you not
a child, and sillier than a child, to think
that I should tell you anything? There's not
a torture or device of any kind
which Zeus can use to make me speak these things,   990
till these atrocious shackles have been loosed.
So let him hurl his smoky lightning flame,
and throw into turmoil all things in the world,
with white-winged snowflakes and deep bellowing
thunder beneath the earth: he shall not bend me   995
by all of this to tell him who is fated
to drive him from his tyranny.

HERMES

Think, here and now, if this seems to your interest.

PROMETHEUS

I have already thought—and laid my plans.

HERMES

Bring your proud heart to recognize discretion—
O foolish spirit—in the face of ruin.   1000

PROMETHEUS

You're annoying me pointlessly, as if you were
advising the waves. Let it not cross your mind
that any fear of Zeus will make me turn
womanish-minded, or that I shall entreat
the one I hate so greatly, with prayerful hands,   1005
to loose me from my chains: I am far from that.

HERMES

I have said too much already—so I think—
and said it all in vain: you are not softened;
your purpose is not dented by my prayers.
You're like a colt new-broken, with the bit   1010
clenched in its teeth, fighting against the reins,
and bolting. You are far too bold and confident

in your weak cleverness. For obstinacy
standing alone is the weakest of all things
in one whose mind is not possessed by wisdom.
Think what a storm, what triple wave of ruin   1015
will rise against you, if you will not hear me,
and there's no escape for you. First this rough crag
with thunder and the lightning bolt the Father
shall split in pieces, and shall hide your body
wrapped in a rocky clasp within its depth;
a vast extent of time you must fulfill   1020
before you see the light again, returning.
Then Zeus's winged hound, the blood-red eagle,
shall butcher tatters of your flesh, a feaster
coming unbidden, every day: your liver
bloodied to blackness will be his repast.   1025
And of this pain do not expect an end
until some god shall show himself successor
to take your tortures for himself, agreeing
to go down to lightless Hades and the shadows
of Tartarus' depths. Bear all this in mind
and so determine. This is no feigned boast   1030
but all too surely spoken. The mouth of Zeus
does not know how to lie, but every word
he brings to fulfilment. Look, you, and reflect
and never think that obstinacy is better
than wise counsel.   1035

CHORUS LEADER
            Hermes seems to us
to speak not altogether out of season.
He bids you quit your obstinacy and seek
a wise good counsel. Listen to him. Shame
it were for one so wise to fall in error.

PROMETHEUS [*chanting*]
Before he told it I knew this message,   1040
and there is no disgrace in suffering

at an enemy's hand, when the hate is mutual.
So, let the curling tendril of fire
from the lightning bolt be sent against me;
let the air be stirred with thunderclaps,　　　　　　　　1045
winds with their blasts convulse the world;
let earth be shaken to her foundations,
roots and all, by the blasts of the storm;
let the waves of the sea confuse the paths
of heavenly stars in a fierce torrent;　　　　　　　　1050
this body of mine, let him hurl it to hell,
to the blackness of Tartarus, with harsh eddies
of fierce necessity! But he shall never
bring me to death.

HERMES [chanting]
Such words are a madman's, a lunatic's plan:
every note's out of tune in his boastful song;　　　　　　1055
his mind is deranged.
　　　　　　But you now, at least,
you, who are so sympathetic with his troubles,
get away from this place, quickly go elsewhere,　　　　　1060
lest the hard and deafening roar of the thunder
destroy your wits.

CHORUS [chanting]
　　　　　　No, say something else
different from this: give me other advice
that might persuade me; this word of yours
was intolerable, that you lured me with.　　　　　　1065
How can you tell us to act like cowards?
I want to endure along with him
what we must endure.
I have learned to hate all traitors; no
disease do I spit on more than treachery.　　　　　　1070

HERMES [chanting]
Well, remember my warning before it happens:
when you are overtaken by ruin don't then

blame fortune—don't say that it was Zeus
that brought you to calamity
quite unforeseen. Do not do this,   1075
but blame yourselves; for now you know
what you are doing, so neither suddenly
nor secretly your own lack of good sense
will have tangled you all in the net of ruin,
past all hope of rescue.

    (Exit Hermes to the side. Sounds of thunder and lightning are heard.)°

PROMETHEUS [*chanting*]
Now it's words no longer: now in truth   1080
the earth is staggered; in its depths the thunder
bellows and roars, the fiery tendrils
of the lightning-flash blaze out, and clouds
carry the dust along in whirls.
All the winds' blasts   1085
dance in a fury one against the other
in violent confusion: sky and sea
are one, all mingled together.
Such is the storm
that comes against me plainly from Zeus   1090
to work its terrors. O holy Mother,
O sky that circling brings light to all,
you see how unjustly I suffer!

         (Exit.)

THE SURVIVING FRAGMENTS OF THE REST OF THE PROMETHEUS TRILOGY

(For discussion of the titles, contents, and order of the plays in the Prometheus trilogy, see Introduction, pp. 168–70)

For *Prometheus Firecarrier* we have only two small pieces of direct evidence: One line from the play is quoted, in Aeschylus fragment 208:

> keeping silent where one should, and speaking to the point.

And an ancient marginal comment (scholion) on *Prometheus Bound* states:

> In the *Firecarrier*, Aeschylus says that Prometheus was bound for 30,000 years.

For *Prometheus Unbound,* however, we are much better informed. The list of characters written in our oldest manuscript of *Prometheus Bound* includes "Earth; Heracles"; and since these two characters do not in fact appear in *Prometheus Bound*, it seems likely that their inclusion here is due to the fact that they did appear in the sequel.

Two ancient marginal comments (scholia) on the text of *Prometheus Bound* refer to "the next play." On line 511 it is stated, "in the next play he is released"; on line 522, that "he is saving his speech for the next play."

Two fragments are quoted (Aeschylus frs. 190 and 191), with an indication that they are chanted by the Titans (who are Prometheus' brothers) at the very beginning of *Prometheus Un-*

bound. Presumably they are the chorus, arriving to witness and speak to Prometheus, somewhat as the daughters of Ocean do in *Prometheus Bound*.

> We have come . . . to view your labors, Prometheus,
> and these chains which you endure . . .

Then the Titans apparently go on to describe their travels all over Europe and Asia, referring (fr. 191) to the River Phasis as "the great double boundary of Europe and Asia." Soon after this, they apparently continue, in Aeschylus fr. 192:

> . . . and the crimson-floored, sacred stream
> of the Red Sea; and the bronze-flashing lake
> next to Ocean, nourishing of all the Ethiopians,
> where the all-seeing Sun ever rests his immortal flesh
> and the weariness of his horses
> with the warm pourings of gentle water.

In response, Prometheus addresses the chorus as follows (fr. 193):

> Race of Titans, kin of my blood,
> begotten of Uranus, look at me bound and chained
> to these rough rocks, like a ship on the roaring seas
> which anxious sailors make fast in fear of nightfall:
> so has Zeus, son of Cronus, fastened me—   5
> and the hand of Hephaestus approved Zeus' will.
> It was he who drove in these wedges with cruel art
> and split open my joints. So, piteously pierced through
> by his skillful workmanship, I occupy
> this outpost of the Furies.
> And now on each alternate deadly day   10
> the servant of Zeus flies grimly down, and starts
> to tear at me with hooked talons, ripping me
> to pieces in his fierce search for food.
> Then amply stuffed, glutted on my rich liver,

he lets out a huge scream, and as he flies away
on high, brushes my gore with feathered tail.   15
But when my gnawed liver has swollen back
to its full size, then greedily back he comes
again to his foul meal. Thus do I feed
this guardian of my grim torture, one
who mangles me alive, in eternal pain.
For, bound, as you see, in Zeus' chains, I cannot   20
ward off the cruel bird from my breast;
bereft of even my own aid, I have to endure
these dreadful torments, and in desire for death
I look around for any end to my troubles—
but I am kept far from death by the power of Zeus.
Indeed, this ancient, grievous pain, grown greater   25
with the horrible years, has now become engrained
in this body of mine, from which the drops,
melted by the heat of the sun, bespatter
the rocks of Caucasus with constant dripping.

From a number of other scattered fragments we gather that Heracles eventually arrived, shot the eagle, and received instructions from Prometheus about his quest for the Apples of the Hesperides and the Cattle of Geryones.

Aeschylus fr. 200 (Heracles speaking):

May hunter Apollo direct the arrow straight!

Aeschylus fr. 201 (Prometheus speaking to or about Heracles):

...this most beloved son of a father hateful to me!

Aeschylus fr. 195 (Prometheus speaking to Heracles):

Keep going straight down this road; and first
you will come to the Northern Winds,
where you must beware of the storming roar,
lest it swirl you up and carry you away
in its wintry blast!

Aeschylus fr. 196 (Prometheus speaking to Heracles):

Then you will come to a people most righteous
and hospitable of all mortals, the Gabioi,
where neither plough nor earth-breaking hoe
cuts the land, but the fields sow themselves
and bear abundant livelihood to mortals.

Aeschylus fr. 197:

In *Prometheus Unbound* Aeschylus says that the River Ister
flows down from the Hyperboreans and the Rhipaean
Mountains.

Aeschylus fr. 199 (Prometheus speaking to Heracles):

You will come to the fearless host of the Ligurians,
where, bold though you are, you will not, I am certain,
find fault with their war making. For it is ordained
that your arrows actually shall fail you there,
and you'll not be able to pick up any stones
from the ground, since the whole area is soft.
But your father, when he sees you in difficulty,
will pity you; he will provide a cloud
and make the land dark with a rain of round stones,
with which you then will pelt the Ligurian army
and easily repel them.

Various additional remarks are made by ancient commentators:

Aeschylus says that Prometheus is released because he
revealed the oracle about Thetis. . . . So the gods settled her
on a mortal husband.

Zeus was pursuing Thetis in the Caucasus to have
intercourse with her; but he was prevented by Prometheus.

Heracles killed the vulture [*sic*], but was afraid to release Prometheus, lest he offend his father.

Aeschylus in *Prometheus Unbound* clearly states that we place crowns on our heads in honor of Prometheus, as recompense for his bondage.

TEXTUAL NOTES

(Line numbers are in some cases only approximate.)

THE PERSIANS

13: Some words are missing, but the general sense is not in doubt.

93-114: The order of stanzas is uncertain: strophe and antistrophe C are written in the manuscripts as lines 102-13, but many modern editors transpose them here (to follow line 92) because of the sense.

237: The order of lines here is uncertain.

675-80: The text here is uncertain, but the general sense is not in doubt.

732: Text uncertain.

767: Some editors transpose this line to follow "brought peace to all he cared for," so as to refer to Cyrus.

859-60: Text uncertain.

922-1074: The rest of the play consists of a sustained lament (*thrênos*) sung antiphonally by Xerxes and the chorus. The language is heavily repetitive and includes many onomatopoeic exclamations of misery, here translated simply as "Oh" or "Ah." The words were obviously subsidiary to the music, choreography, and gestures. Furthermore, the text is not well preserved. In some cases the assignment of the sung phrases to Xerxes, to the chorus, or to both together is unclear or disputed. The translation in what follows should therefore be understood as being quite sketchy as a record of the scene's overall meaning and impact.

935: Text uncertain.

944-45: Text uncertain.

980: Text uncertain.

981–82: A name is missing here.

1008: Text very uncertain.

1072: Two lines appear to be missing here.

THE SEVEN AGAINST THEBES

CHARACTERS: The medieval manuscripts include among the list of characters Antigone, Ismene, and a Herald. These three appear toward the end of the play, as preserved in the manuscripts. Most modern editors believe, however, that the whole scene involving the Herald is a later addition to Aeschylus' play, and that the lines assigned by the manuscripts in a previous scene to Antigone and Ismene were originally composed by Aeschylus to be sung or chanted by the chorus, and only later adapted to be sung by these two sisters. See further the notes to lines 822–31, 847, 861–74, 875, 1005–78.

78–89: The text is uncertain in many places, though the general sense is not in doubt.

121: Text uncertain.

132–48: The text is uncertain in many places, but the general sense is clear.

217: The sense of this line and the next is uncertain.

277: This line is deleted by many modern editors.

283: The phrase "in gallant style" is doubtful; the correct reading is uncertain.

356: The text is uncertain, but the general sense is not in doubt.

359: Text and interpretation are uncertain.

426–27: Many editors delete this line and a half.

514–20: The order of lines is uncertain here, and several editors have chosen to delete two or three lines as well. But the general sense is not in doubt.

576–78: The text is doubtful in several places, and some editors delete one or more lines.

584: The text and meaning here are uncertain.

590: Some editors read instead "brandishing calmly his brazen shield."

633–34: Some editors delete these lines, to read: "He prays to be proclaimed the conqueror of this land and adds a paean of triumph at its overthrow; and he asks to close in fight with you."

703: The sense of this line is uncertain.

783: The text of this line and its sense are quite uncertain.

792: A line appears to be missing here: the text says only "children raised from mothers."

803–9: The manuscripts contain one extra line, which most editors delete (804 "The city is saved, but the two princes . . . ," almost identical to line 812). Then a pair of lines appears to have dropped out between 808 and 809.

813–14: These two lines have been transposed here by modern editors. In the manuscripts they follow line 821.

822–31: Most editors regard these lines as being not Aeschylus' work but a later interpolation, together with 861-73 and the whole ending of the play (1005-74). See Introduction, p. 66.

847 (stage direction): If the ending of the play transmitted in the manuscripts is genuinely by Aeschylus (most editors regard this as unlikely), then at this point, along with the attendants carrying the dead bodies of the two brothers, Antigone and Ismene also enter. (See Introduction, p. 66.)

853: Text uncertain: possibly, "sorrows take up residence with more sorrows."

861–74: Most editors think these lines were not written by Aeschylus but were added later, when the play was restaged for an audience by now familiar with Sophocles' *Antigone*: see Introduction, p. 66.

875, 878, etc.: Two different speakers (singers) deliver all of 875-1004 in alternation, as a ritualized lamentation duet. The manuscripts indicate that these singers are the two sisters, Antigone and Ismene; but most editors are agreed that all these lines were originally composed to be sung by the chorus, now divided into two groups. (Similarly 1054-78, whether or not those lines are by Aeschylus.)

1005–78: All or almost all of the lines of this final scene as presented in the medieval manuscripts are agreed by most editors to be a post-Aeschylean addition to the play. We do not know how Aeschylus' own version concluded; but probably the antiphonal lamentation by the chorus continued to the end (with no Herald, and no speaking roles for Antigone or Ismene).

1047: The text is uncertain, and this is no more than a guess at the meaning.

70: Text uncertain: perhaps "my sun-burnt cheek."

80-82: Text very uncertain.

88-90, 93-95: Some editors think that these lines have been accidentally transposed in the manuscript tradition.

110: Text very uncertain.

121-23: The text of these lines is extremely uncertain, and the sense unclear.

175-76: The refrain ("O Zeus! Poor Io . . . ," as in 162-66) is not written here in the manuscript, but most editors think it was supposed to be repeated, just as the previous refrains were (117-20 = 127-30; and 141-43 = 150-52).

205-10: The order of these lines appears to have been jumbled in the manuscript; most editors rearrange them as here.

295-317: Throughout this passage, the order of lines and assignment of speakers are very uncertain, and in at least two places it looks as if a line has dropped out from the manuscript. Most editors agree that the lines should be arranged so that King Pelasgus generally asks questions while the Chorus Leader supplies information and narrative details.

330-31: Text uncertain.

363-64: A few words are missing in the manuscript, but the general sense is clear.

515: The text is uncertain. Some editors read: "Women always feel excessive fear."

575: A line is missing here in the manuscript, but the general sense is not in doubt.

628-29: Text and sense are very doubtful.

635: Text uncertain: this is a probable emendation of the manuscript's "a danceless cry."

661-62: The word "strife" is missing in the manuscript and is supplied by modern editors.

667-68: Text very uncertain.

682: Text uncertain.

773: A line appears to have dropped out here; the translation conveys the general sense.

784: Text very uncertain.

808-10: The text is extremely uncertain.

825-35: At this point the text in our manuscript is hopelessly defective: only bits of separate words, or nonsense syllables, can be read. It is unclear how much has been lost from Aeschylus' original and whether the garbled nature of the language reflects a kind of "broken Greek" uttered by these Egyptian sailors or whether it is simply an accident of the textual transmission.

836-902: The text continues to be seriously defective throughout this passage. At no point does the manuscript specify whether a "Chorus of Egyptians" or a "Herald" is the speaker (see 872), and editors have disagreed as to how all these lines should be divided between the main chorus and the other singing characters.

850-51: Text and interpretation are extremely uncertain.

859: Text and sense are very uncertain.

872: From here on, the lines from the Egyptian interlocutor are in trimeters—i.e., spoken, not sung: so most editors have concluded that this is now a herald speaking, rather than an Egyptian chorus as previously.

873-75, 882-84: Some editors transpose these three-line speeches from the Herald, on the grounds that they then better fit the dramatic context.

876-881: The translation of this whole stanza is little more than guesswork; the transmitted text is largely unintelligible.

895-900: Text and interpretation extremely uncertain.

905, 908: These lines have been switched (as here) by most modern editors, since the Herald's responses seem to imply this order.

941: This last phrase is missing in the manuscript, and has been supplied by modern editors.

954: The manuscripts have a masculine form here, which would mean "attended by friendly [sc: Argive] escorts"; see note on 1034-73 below.

977-79: These lines are rejected by some editors as a later interpolation.

988: One or more lines appear to have been lost after this line.

1034-73: Scholars disagree as to whether this secondary chorus is made up of male Argive citizens (the escorts provided by King Pelasgus) or of female servants of the Danaids. If it is the latter, it is surprising that so little mention has been made of them previously. Some scholars have suggested that the play was revised after Aeschylus' death and this second chorus added.

PROMETHEUS BOUND

128: The text seems to indicate that the chorus enters flying, presumably either onto the roof of the stage building or by means of some kind of "machine" (*mêchanê*) that allows them to hover in the air. Modern scholars have disagreed whether or not to take these indications literally, and if so, where and how to envisage the staging of this unparalleled aerial entry of twelve or fifteen chorus members.

283: If the chorus were hovering in the air during the opening scene, they probably depart now, to reappear at ground level at 397. It is notable that they make no contact at all with Ocean (their father) in the scene that follows now, so they are probably not present.

354: Text uncertain.

397: Presumably the chorus reenters at this point into the orchestra, from the side. See note to line 283.

410: A word or two has dropped out here; "your fall" is a modern supplement.

430: A line may be missing here.

463: "Pack saddles" is an emendation accepted by most scholars for the manuscript reading "with their bodies."

541: Text uncertain.

543: Text uncertain.

558: The phrase "with your gifts" is deleted by many editors, for the meter.

760: Text uncertain. Some editors emend to read, "Since things are truly thus, you may rejoice."

792: Some editors read instead, "crossing the waves of the sea." The "waveless sea" means the dry steppes.

848: Some editors think a line has dropped out here, in which the impregnation of Io by Zeus is mentioned as well.

860: Text uncertain. Some editors think a line has dropped out here too.

880: Text uncertain.

895: There are several textual uncertainties in this stanza, but the general sense is not in doubt.

970: A line spoken by Prometheus seems to be missing before this one.

1079: How the ending was staged—whether or not the chorus departed before Prometheus' final words and whether and how Prometheus exited— is unclear.

GLOSSARY

Achaea, Achaean: (1) a region (and its inhabitants) in the Peloponnese. In Homer and tragedy "Achaean" is often used as another name for "Greek" in general; in *The Seven against Thebes* it refers to the Argives. (2) Achaea Phthiotis was a region in northeast Greece, on the north shore of the Malian Gulf in southern Thessaly.

Achelous: the longest river in Greece; rising in Epirus, it empties into the Corinthian Gulf. "Acheloian" was used by the poets to mean "fresh water."

Acheron: a river or lake in the underworld.

Actor: Theban champion, son of Oenops; brother of Hyperbius; fights against and kills Parthenopaeus at the Northern gate.

Adeues: a leader of the Persian army.

Adrastus: king of Argos; father of Argeia (Polynices' wife).

Aedoneus: another name for Hades, god of the underworld.

Aegean: the sea that separates mainland Greece from the mainland of Anatolia (modern-day Turkey).

Aethiops: Ethiopian, often referring rather vaguely to any region to the extreme south.

Aetna: volcano in Sicily under which the monster Typhon is imprisoned.

Agabatas: a leader of the Persian army.

Agbatana: capital city of Media, north of Sousa (in modern-day Iran).

Ajax's isle: another name for Salamis, the homeland of Ajax, a Greek hero at Troy.

Amazons: a legendary race of militaristic man-hating women, descended from Ares, thought to live by the Black Sea. They fought against Heracles; they also invaded Attica after Theseus abducted their queen Antiope, but were eventually defeated.

Amistres or Amistris: a leader of the Persian army.

Amphiaraus: one of the seven Argive champions; a seer who did not want to fight against Thebes, but was convinced by his wife, Eriphyle, to do so.

Amphion: cofounder of Thebes, with his twin brother Zethus; he was a lyre-player, and built the city's walls by moving the stones with his music;

husband of Niobe, Tantalus' daughter; his tomb was located northeast of the Theban citadel.

Amphistreus: a leader of the Persian army.

Anchares: a leader of the Persian army.

Andros: a small island in the central Aegean Sea.

Antigone: daughter of Oedipus and Jocasta; sister of Ismene, Polynices, and Eteocles.

Aphrodite: goddess of erotic desire; associated closely with the cities of Paphos, Solus, and Salamis (all on Cyprus).

Apia, Apian land: the Peloponnesus and Argos, named for the seer Apis, a legendary early king of Argos.

Apis: (1) a seer, healer, and legendary early king of Argos; (2) an Egyptian bull-god sometimes associated with Epaphus.

Apollo: son of Leto and Zeus; brother of Artemis; god of prophecy, healing, music, and archery.

Arabia: region near the upper Euphrates (modern Iraq), or perhaps in the Pontus region on the southern coast of the Black Sea.

Arabus: a leader of the Persian army; one of the Magi.

Arcadia: a region in the center of the Peloponnesus in southern Greece.

Arcteus: a commander in the Persian army.

Ares: god of war.

Argestes: a leader of the Persian army.

Argive(s): of/from Argos; the citizens of Argos.

Argos: a major city in the Peloponnese located in the southern region of the Argive plain. The name is often used interchangeably with Mycenae, which was nearby and in the classical period barely existed as a town.

Argus: the "all-seeing" and many-eyed herdsman whom Hera appointed to guard Io after she has been transformed into a cow; killed by Hermes at Zeus' command.

Arimaspians: mythical one-eyed people who live by the gold-bearing river Pluto in the Far East.

Ariomardus: a leader in the Persian army; governor of Egyptian Thebes.

Arsames: a leader of the Persian army; governor of Egyptian Memphis.

Artabes: a Bactrian leader in the Persian army.

Artaphrenes: (1) a leader of the Persian army, possibly a regional ruler; (2) a Persian nobleman, brother of Darius; sometimes confused by the Greeks with Intaphrenes, who helped Darius first gain the Persian throne in a palace coup.

Artembares: a leader of the Persian army.

Artemis: daughter of Leto and Zeus; sister of Apollo; goddess of the hunt.

Asia: Asia Minor or Anatolia (modern-day Turkey).

Asopus: the main river in Boeotia; it rises on Mount Cithaeron and flows through Plataea into the Euripus Strait.

Astacus: father of Melanippus, one of the Theban defenders against the Seven.

Astaspes: a leader of the Persian army.

Athamas: mythical father of Phrixus and Helle; husband of Nephele.

Athena: daughter of Zeus; goddess of wisdom and military strategy.

Athens, Athenians: Athens was the largest Greek city-state, located in Attica (east-central Greece). The Athenians were "Ionian" Greeks, in their language and cultural traditions.

Atlas: brother of Prometheus; he stands in the Far West eternally supporting the sky on his shoulders.

Axius: the large river which flows through Macedonia and into the Thermaic Gulf (near modern-day Thessaloniki).

Babylon: a large Mesopotamian city located between the Tigris and Euphrates Rivers (modern-day Al-Hillah, Iraq)

Bacchant, Bacchanal: a frenzied follower of Dionysus (Bacchus); also called maenad.

Bactrian: Bactria was a region in central Asia, northeast of Persia, covering a territory which is now eastern Iran, Afghanistan, and southern Russia.

Batanochus: a leader of the Persian army, and father of the "king's eye," an important court dignitary.

Belus: son of Libya and Poseidon; king of Egypt; father of Egyptus and Danaus.

Bibline hills: exact location unknown; somewhere in Egypt.

Blessed Ones: another term for the gods.

Boeotia: a region in east-central Greece; Thebes and Plataea were two of its major cities.

Bolbe: a large lake (modern Vólvi) in eastern Macedonia connected to the Strymon Gulf.

Bosphorus: sometimes used as another name for the Hellespont, the strait connecting Anatolia (modern-day Turkey) and Greece. The true Bosphorus, however, was the strait dividing Europe from Asia at Byzantium/ Chalcedon (modern-day Istanbul). *See too* Cow's Ford.

Cadmeans: citizens of Thebes, called so after Cadmus.

Cadmus: son of Agenor; brother of Europa; father of Polydorus, Agave, Autonoë, Ino, and Semele; originally a Phoenician, then founder and first king of Thebes.

Canobus (or Canopus): city in Egypt located on the Nile Delta on the edge of modern-day Alexandria.

Capaneus: one of the Argive champions against Thebes; fights at Electra's gates; Zeus kills him with a thunderbolt.

Caress: Epaphus' name means "touching" or "caress."

Caucasus, Caucasian Mountains: a range of mountains (in *Prometheus Bound*) of uncertain location, apparently somewhere between the Black Sea and the Caspian Sea; perhaps the Rhipaean Mountains (modern-day Ural Mountains).

Cerchnea: river that ran beside the village of the same name, located southwest of Argos.

Chalyb, Chalybes: member(s) of the Chalybians, legendary ironworkers who were thought to live either on the north shore of the Black Sea (in Scythia), or in Anatolia.

Chios: a large island in the northeast Aegean Sea, close to the coast of Anatolia (modern-day Turkey).

Chrysa: a small town near Troy.

Cilician: referring to Cilicia, a region on the southern coast of Anatolia (modern-day Turkey), east of Pamphylia, northeast of Cyprus.

Cimmeria: the Crimea, the large peninsula in the northern Black Sea.

Cissa: region (modern-day Khuzestan) in southwestern Iran.

Cisthene: plain or mountain to the east, perhaps in Libya or Anatolia.

Cnidus: an island in the southern Aegean Sea.

Colchis, Colchian: region (and its people) located at the eastern end of the Black Sea (modern-day Georgia) around the mouth of the Phasis River (modern-day Rioni River).

Cow's Ford: the Bosphorus, where Io crossed from Europe into Asia; named from the Greek words for "ox, cow" and "passage."

Cronus: husband of Rhea; father of Zeus, Poseidon, Hera, and other Olympian deities; one of the Titans. When Zeus and the younger generation of gods defeated the Titans, Cronus was imprisoned forever in Tartarus.

Cychraean: Cychreus was a mythical hero of Salamis; son of Poseidon and the nymph Salamis. The "Cychraean shores" are the shores of Salamis.

Cypris: another name for Aphrodite; the island Cyprus was sacred to her.

Cyprus, Cypriots: a large island in the eastern Mediterranean to the south of modern-day Turkey (and its inhabitants).

Cyrus (the Great): founder of the Persian Empire (ruled 559–529 BCE) and of the Achaemenid dynasty; father of Cambyses.

Dadakes: a leader of the Persian army.

Danaids: the fifty daughters of Danaus.

Danaus: a descendent of Io; son of Belus and Achiroe, daughter of Nile; twin brother of Egyptus; father of fifty daughters (the Danaids), he flees with them to Argos so that they will not be forced to marry his brother's fifty sons. Later he becomes king of Argos.

Darius: king of Persia (ruled 521–486 BCE); husband of Atossa and father of Xerxes. His actual Iranian name was Darayavaush.

Diaixis: a leader of the Persian army.

Dirce: river to the west of Thebes.

Dodona: city in Thesprotia in Epirus (northwestern Greece), west of the Pindus Mountains; location of the most famous oracle of Zeus.

Dorian: Dorian Greeks (concentrated especially in the Peloponnese) shared linguistic and other cultural traits that distinguished them from Aeolian and Ionian Greeks. "Dorian" was sometimes used more generally as another name for Spartan.

Dotamas: a leader of the Persian army.

Earth: in Greek, Gaia or Gê; wife of Ouranos; mother of Prometheus and of the Titans.

Egyptus: a descendant of Io; son of Belus and Achiroe, daughter of the Nile; twin brother of Danaus; king of Egypt. Father of fifty sons whom he wishes betrothed to his brother's fifty daughters.

Electra's gate: name of one of the seven gates of Thebes.

Enyo: goddess of war.

Epaphus: son of Zeus and Io; he became king of Egypt. His name means "touching" or "caress."

Erasinus: a river, and river god, of the Argive plain. The river rises near Lake Stymphalus in Arcadia and flows south past Argos.

Eros: god of sexual desire.

Eteocles: son (and brother) of Oedipus; son of Jocasta; brother of Antigone, Ismene, and Polynices; ruler of Thebes briefly after Oedipus' death.

Eteoclus: Argive champion against Thebes; he fights against and is killed by Megareus at the gate of Neïs.

Ethiopian: Ethiopia was the region to the south of Egypt (including modern Sudan and Ethiopia).

Fates: three divinities who are sometimes imagined as collaborating to assign every person and thing its due "portion" (in Greek, *Moira*). But more often "fate" is regarded as a more nebulous force, rather than personified.

Father Ocean: *see* Oceanus.

Fury: female avenging spirit concerned especially with bloodguilt; in Greek *Erinys*.

Gorgon(s): three female monsters, sisters: Medusa ("ruler"), Sthenno ("strength"), and Euryale ("wide-leaper"); their gaze turned men to stone.

Gorgona: the land, perhaps Libya or Anatolia, where the Gorgons live. *See* Cisthene.

Hades: god of and the name for the underworld; brother of Zeus and Poseidon; husband of Persephone. Sometimes "Hades" is used to mean simply "death."

Halys: a large river in eastern Anatolia (modern-day Turkey).

Hecate-Artemis: Artemis, daughter of Zeus and Leto and twin sister of Apollo, was the protector of women during childbirth. Hecate, originally a distinct goddess, sometimes comes to be associated, even identified, with Artemis.

Hellas: Greece.

Helle: daughter of Athamas and Nephele; she drowned in the strait connecting Anatolia (Turkey) and Greece, which was therefore named the Hellespont ("strait of Helle").

Hephaestus: god of fire and metalwork.

Hera: sister and wife of Zeus; queen of the gods.

Hermes: son of Zeus and Maia; god of contests, travel, stealth, heralds; he escorts dead souls to Hades.

Hesione: daughter of Oceanus; wife of Prometheus.

Hippomedon: Argive champion against Thebes; father of Polydorus; he fights against and is killed by Ismarus at the gate that neighbors Onca Athena.

Homoloian gate: one of Thebes' seven gates, attacked by Amphiaraus.

Hyperbius: Theban champion; son of Oenops; brother of Actor; he fights against Hippomedon.

Hystaechmes: a leader of the Persian army.

Ikaros: a small island in the southern Aegean Sea, off the coast of Anatolia.

Imaeus: a leader of the Persian army.

Inachus: a river and river-god of the Argive plain; king of Argos; father of Io. The river flows past Argos on the north side of the city.

Insolence: "Hybristes," likely an imaginary river; or else either the Araxes, located to the east of the Black Sea, or the Hypanis (modern-day Kuban River), which flows from the Caucasus into the Sea of Azov (ancient Lake Maeotis).

Io: daughter of Inachus; priestess of Hera in Argos. She was amorously pursued by Zeus, who transformed her into a cow to hide his amour from his wife Hera. But Hera was not fooled, and appointed the "all-seeing" Argus to watch over Io. When Argus was slain by Hermes, Io began wandering wildly, plagued by a gadfly sent by Hera, and ultimately ended up in Egypt; here, from Zeus' "touch," she conceived Epaphus, whose descendants became the ruling dynasty in Egypt.

Ionia, Ionian: the central section of the west coast of Anatolia (modern-day Turkey), colonized by Greeks. Ionian Greeks (including the Athenians) shared linguistic and other cultural traits that distinguished them from Aeolian and Dorian Greeks. Sometimes "Ionian" is used to mean simply "Greek" (as opposed to, e.g., "Persian"). "Ionian songs" refers to the laments common in Anatolia.

Ionian (sea): the sea between Italy and Greece, south of the Adriatic Sea.

Ismene: daughter of Oedipus and Jocasta; sister of Antigone, Polynices, and Eteocles.

Ismenus: river which flows from the foothills of Mount Cithaeron past Thebes.

Knidos (or Cnidos): an island in the southern Aegean Sea.

Laius: son of Labdacus; husband of Jocasta and father of Oedipus; king of Thebes; unknowingly killed by Oedipus.

Lasthenes: Theban champion who fights against Amphiaraus.

Lemnos: an island in the northern Aegean Sea.

Lerna: marshy region just south of Argos.

Lesbos: an island in the northeast Aegean Sea, close to the coast of Anatolia (modern-day Turkey).

Leto: mother of Apollo and Artemis, by Zeus.

Libya: personification of the region Libya; daughter of Epaphus and Memphis. She was raped by Poseidon and gave birth to Belus and Agenor.

Libyans: the inhabitants of Libya, the region of North Africa.

Lilaeus: a leader of the Persian army.

Locria (or Locris): a region in central Greece, next to Phocis.

Loxias: epithet of Apollo often used in place of his name; the name means "crooked."

Lycian: referring to Apollo.

Lydian: Lydia was a region in west-central Anatolia (modern-day Turkey); its main city was Sardis (modern-day Sart).

Lyrnaean: Lyrna, or Lyrnessa, is apparently a town near Troy inhabited by Cilicians.

Lythimnas: a leader of the Persian army.

Macedonia: the region of northern Greece north of Thessaly and west of Thrace.

Maeotis: large lake northeast of the Crimean Peninsula (modern-day Sea of Azov).

Magian: the Magi were a Medo-Persian tribe, renowned for their religious expertise.

Magnesia: the northeastern region of Thessaly, in northern Greece.

Malian Gulf: the bay in east-central Greece into which the Spercheius River flows.

Marathon: a small town in Attica, twenty miles northeast of Athens. In the Battle of Marathon (490 BCE) the Athenians, aided by the Plataeans, defeated the much larger Persian army in an infantry encounter, effectively ending the first Persian invasion of Greece. Aeschylus is said to have fought in that battle.

Mardia: the Mardians were a nomadic Persian tribe.

Mardon: a commander in the Persian army, from Lydia.

Mardos: a usurper king of Persia, assassinated by Darius and Artaphrenes or Intaphrenes. (Herodotus calls him Smerdis. His actual Persian name was Gaumata.)

Mariandynian: from a region in northwest Anatolia (modern-day Turkey) famous for its musical dirges.

Masistres: a leader of the Persian army.

Matallus: a leader of the Persian army.

Median: the Medes were the inhabitants of Media, the region in the northwest portion of modern-day Iran; after the rise to power of Cyrus the Great, the Medes and Persians were closely associated.

Medus: the legendary founder of the Medes.

Megabates: a leader of the Persian army.

Megareus: Theban champion; son of Creon; he fights against and kills Eteoclus.

Melanippus: Theban champion; son of Astacus; he defends the Proetid gate against Tydeus.

Memphis: (1) a city in Egypt located to the south of modern-day Cairo; (2) a leader of the Persian army.

Metis: apparently another name for Procne, wife of Tereus.

Metrogathes: a commander of Lydian troops in the Persian army.

Might (Greek *Kratos*): son of the River Styx; with Violence, he serves as Zeus' enforcer.

Molossian plain: region in Epirus, northwestern Greece.

Muses: daughters of Mnemosyne and Zeus, associated with all forms of cultural, especially artistic, poetic, and musical, excellence.

Mykonos: a small island in the central Aegean Sea.

Mysian: Mysia is a region in northwest Anatolia (modern-day Turkey), north of Lydia. "Mysian laments" refer to an Eastern form of dirge.

Naupactus: a town in the region of Aetolia; it is located on a bay on the north side of the straits of Lepanto, near the Gulf of Corinth.

Naxos: an island in the central Aegean Sea.

Nile: the main river in Egypt.

Nilotis: the Nile Delta, in Egypt.

Ocean, or Oceanus: son of Ouranos and Earth (Gaia); a Titan; brother and husband of Tethys; god of the waters; father of the Oceanids.

Oebares: a leader of the Persian army.

Oecleides: patronymic meaning "son of Oecles," referring to Amphiaraus.

Oecles: father of Amphiaraus.

Oedipus: son of Laius and Jocasta; husband of Jocasta; father (and brother) of Antigone, Ismene, Polynices, and Eteocles. King of Thebes.

Oenops: father of Actor and Hyperbius, two Theban defenders against the Seven.

Olympian (gods): the twelve main gods (Aphrodite, Apollo, Ares, Artemis, Athena, Demeter, Dionysus, Hephaestus, Hera, Hermes, Poseidon, Zeus) who have their home on Mount Olympus.

Onca Athena, Onca Pallas: one of Thebes' seven gates, named for the sanctuary of Onca Athena that stood near it.

Ouranos: husband and brother of Earth (Gaia); his name means "sky"; father of Cronus and the Titans.

Padshah: an (alleged) Phrygian word for "king."

Paeoni: the tribe who occupied Paeonia, a region in northern Thrace.

Palaechthon: father of Pelasgus; his name means "ancient earth."

Pallas: epithet of Athena.

Pamphylia: a region on the southern coast of Anatolia (modern-day Turkey), west of Cilicia.

Pan: a woodland god who was worshipped throughout Greece, and especially on Salamis.

Pangaeon: a large mountain in western Thrace, bordering on Macedonia.

Paphos: a city on the island of Cyprus.

Paros: a small island in the central Aegean Sea.

Parthenopaeus: Argive champion against Thebes; son of Atalanta and either Melanion or Ares; he fights against and is killed by Actor at the Northern gate. His name is derived from the word for "maiden, virgin."

Parthus: a leader of the Persian army.

Pegastagon: an Egyptian commander in the Persian army.

Pelagon: a leader of the Persian army.

Pelasgian earth or land: Argos, founded by Pelasgus.

Pelasgians: in legend, the earliest inhabitants of Greece.

Pelasgus: son of Palaechthon; founder and king of Argos.

Pentheus: a king of Thebes who resisted Dionysus and was torn apart by Bacchants as a punishment (the subject of Euripides' *Bacchae*).

Perrhaebi, Perrhaebians: a tribe that lived in northern Thessaly.

Perseus: son of Zeus and Danae; mythical founder of Mycenae; slayer of Medusa. His son with Andromeda, Perses, was supposed to have been the founder of the Persian race.

Persians: the people of Persia (modern-day Iran). The term is often used loosely by the Greeks to include Medes and other peoples contained within the Persian Empire (which embraced most of the world from Macedonia to Egypt, from Palestine and the Arabian peninsula across Mesopotamia and all the way to India).

Pharandakas: a leader of the Persian army.

Pharnouchus: a leader of the Persian army.

Phocis: a region in central Greece near Delphi, west of Boeotia.

Phoebus: an epithet of Apollo, meaning "bright."

Phoenician: Phoenicia was the region on the Levantine coast of the eastern Mediterranean (modern-day Lebanon, Syria, and Israel). Phoenicians were renowned for their naval expertise and maritime trade.

Phorcys: god of the sea; son of Pontus and Gaia; husband of Ceto; father of the Gorgons and the Graeae (the "swan-formed hags").

Phrygia, Phrygian: Phrygia was the northwest-central region of Anatolia (modern-day Turkey).

Pindus: large mountain range in what is today northern Greece and southern Albania.

Plataea: a town in southern Boeotia located between Mount Cithaeron and the Asopus River; the Greek (Spartan-led) infantry victory in the Battle of Plataea (479 BCE) effectively ended Xerxes' campaign against Greece.

Pluto: (1) another name for Hades; (2) an imaginary river in the Far East.

Polynices: son of Oedipus and Jocasta; brother of Eteocles, Ismene, and Antigone; he married Argeia, daughter of Adrastus, king of Argos, and waged war on Thebes seeking to claim the kingdom for himself. The name in Greek means "much strife."

Polyphontes: Theban champion against the Seven; he opposes Capaneus at Electra's gate.

Pontus: the Black Sea.

Poseidon: god of the sea; brother of Zeus and Hades.

Proetid gate: one of Thebes' seven gates, where Melanippus faces Tydeus.

Prometheus: a Titan, son of Iapetus and (in *Prometheus Bound*) of Gaia-Themis; he stole fire from the gods and gave it to mankind, for which he was punished by Zeus. His name means "forethought."

Propontis: the Sea of Marmara. To the east, the Bosphorus Strait connects it to the Black Sea; to the west, the Dardanelles Strait connects it to the Aegean Sea.

Psammis: a leader of the Persian army.

Pytho (Pythian): another name for Delphi, Apollo's sanctuary in central Greece; the name comes from the serpent Python whom Apollo slew there. The Delphic prophetess was given the title Pythia.

Rhea: wife of Cronus; mother of Zeus, Poseidon, and other gods. The Gulf of Rhea is a name for the Adriatic Sea, between Greece and Italy.

Rhodos (Rhodes): an island in the southern Aegean Sea, close to the coast of Anatolia.

Salamis, Salaminian: (1) a small island in the Saronic Gulf about ten miles west of Athens. The Battle of Salamis (480 BCE) was a naval battle fought between the Persian invading force and an alliance of Greek cities led by the Athenians. "An island fronting Salamis" is Psyttaleia. (2) A city on the island of Cyprus.

Salmydessus: a city in Thrace on the Black Sea, about sixty miles northwest from the Hellespont.

Samos: a large island in the southeast Aegean Sea, close to the coast of Anatolia (modern-day Turkey).

Sardis: capital city (modern-day Sart) of the Lydian kingdom in western Anatolia (modern-day Turkey), located at the foot of Mount Tmolus.

Sarpedon: a son of Zeus; king of Lycia, a region in southern Anatolia (modern-day Turkey) to the west of Pamphylia; Sarpedon's tomb is at the mouth of the river Calycadnus in Cilicia.

Scythia, Scythians: the name given to the wild lands and the inhabitants of the Black Sea region northeast of mainland Greece (modern-day Bulgaria, Romania, Ukraine). The Scythians are frequently noted for their savagery, nomadism, and archery.

Seisames: (1) father of Batanochus and grandfather of the "king's eye," an important Persian dignitary; (2) a leader of the Mysian contingent in the Persian army.

Seualces: a leader in the Persian army.

Sicily: large island off the western tip of the "boot" of Italy.

Sidonian: Sidon is a Phoenician city on the coast of what is today Lebanon. The Phoenicians were renowned sailors and merchants.

Silenia: the name given to a stretch of Salamis' coastline, probably one side of the Cynosura Peninsula on the eastern end of the island.

Soli: a city on the island of Cyprus.

Sousa: large city (modern-day Shush) located east of the Tigris River in the Cissa region (modern-day Iran). One of the capital cities of the Persian Empire.

Sousas: a leader of the Persian army.

Sousiscanes: (1) an Egyptian leader in the Persian army; (2) a leader of the Persian army.

Sousthenes: a leader of the Persian army.

Sown Men: the men who sprang from the earth fully armed when Cadmus sowed the ground with the teeth of the dragon he slew at Thebes; legendary ancestors of several of the leading families at Thebes.

Spercheian: the river Spercheius in east-central Greece flows into the Malian Gulf.

Sphinx: mythological monster who guarded the entrance to Thebes and asked passersby a riddle. Those who failed to answer correctly were killed. She was defeated and killed by Oedipus, who solved her riddle.

Strait of Helle: the Hellespont (*see* Helle).

Strymon: a river in Macedonia which flows into the Strymon Gulf at Amphipolis. It was often regarded as marking the border between Greece and Thrace.

Syennesis: a Cimmerian leader in the Persian army.

Syria: a region in the Levant, roughly equivalent to modern-day Syria.

Tartarus: the lowest level of Hades, to which the most serious evildoers are consigned.

Tenagon: a Bactrian leader in the Persian army.

Tenos: a small island in the central Aegean Sea.

Tereus: son of Ares; husband of Procne (or Metis), father of Itys; king of Thrace. He raped his wife's sister (Philomela) and cut out her tongue so she could not tell anyone what had happened. Procne exacted terrible revenge.

Tethys: daughter of Ouranos and Earth (Gaia); a Titan; wife and sister of Ocean; mother of all rivers.

Teuthras: a city in Mysia, a region in northwest Anatolia (modern-day Turkey).

Tharybis: a leader of the Persian army, from Lyrn(ess)a.

Thebes: (1) a large city in Boeotia, central Greece; (2) a city in Egypt about 500 miles south of the Nile Delta.

Themis: primeval personification of custom, right, and established law; usually considered to be a daughter of Gaia and Ouranos, and so a sister of Cronus and the other Titans. In *Prometheus Bound* she is said to be the mother of Prometheus, and is also identified with Gaia.

Themiscyra: region on the southern coast of the Black Sea; one supposed home of the Amazons.

Thermodon: river in northern Turkey (modern-day Terme).

Thesprotian: Thesprotis was a region in Epirus, northwestern Greece.

Thessaly: a large region in northeast-central Greece, south of Macedonia.

Thrace, Thracian: an extensive region (and its inhabitants) to the northeast covering what is today northeastern Greece, southeastern Bulgaria, and northwest Turkey.

Titan, Titans: the sons and daughters of Ouranos and Earth; they are the generation before the Olympian gods; their leader was Cronus.

Tmolus: the mountain in Lydia at whose base Sardis is located.

Tolmus: a leader of the Persian army.

Tydeus: Argive champion against Thebes; son of Oeneus and Periboea; father of Diomedes; he fought against Melanippus at the Proetid gate.

Typho(n): monstrous child of Tartarus and Gaia, who waged war on Zeus to avenge the defeat of the Titans; he is eternally imprisoned under Mount Aetna in Sicily.

Violence (Greek *Bia*): child of the River Styx, who, with Might, serves as Zeus' enforcer.

War: Ares, the god of war.

Way of Helle: the Hellespont.

wolf god: Apollo (perhaps from his cult epithet *Lykeios*, though the etymology is uncertain).

Xanthes: a leader of the Persian army.

Xerxes: son of Darius and Atossa; king of Persia and leader of the military expedition against Greece in 480–479 BCE.

Zeus: son of Cronus; king of the Olympian gods.